INSPIRING SPECIAL NEEDS STORIES

RENA YEAGER

Inspiring Special Needs Stories

By Rena Yeager

Published by Alaska Dreams Publishing
www.alaskadp.com

First eBook Edition October 2020
First Print Edition October 2020
PRINT ISBN - 13: 978-0-9903454-9-7

Print and eBook versions available.
Please visit www.alaskadp.com for links.

This book is dedicated to my parents,
Ralph and Sherley Yeager—
gone, but forever in my heart.
To Kathy Dodge, my high school English teacher,
who always encouraged me to keep writing.
Most of all, this book is dedicated to the Lord,
as without Him, this book would not have been possible.
I write for His glory.

CONTENTS

STORY FOUR
Lexi

STORY FIVE
Sarah's Song

ACKNOWLEDGMENTS

First and foremost, I would like to acknowledge God for giving me the ability to write, the passion for writing, and for putting the right people in my life to make my dream become a reality.

To a close friend of over 20 years, Sue Jones, who would read my stories, give suggestions, and would often help write scenes.

To Kim Wood, my supervisor and dear friend, who read my stories and encouraged me to keep writing.

To Bob Jacobson, who read my stories and spent many hours mentoring and teaching me what it takes to become a serious writer.

To The Orion Corp. of MN, who hired me in 1995 to work with people with disabilities, who trained me, and through them, I developed a passion for helping people with disabilities. What started out as a job turned into a 25-year career.

To Margo Hansen, a friend and also an author, who was

always willing to answer my questions and encouraged me to follow my dreams.

To all my family and all my friends for being a part of my life, whether I've known you for 50 years or one, you are all so very important to me.

STORY ONE

The Essay Contest

1 - THE ESSAY CONTEST

$\mathcal{W}$hat are you going to write your essay about?" Shaylynne said, as she dropped her books on her desk and sat down on the bed. She lifted Timberwolf, her Yorkie puppy, up onto the bed, and rubbed his ears.

"I don't know," Mataya replied. "What about you?"

"I'm not sure yet." Her friend answered with unmistakable excitement in her voice. "Boy, this is going to be fun. Hey, maybe one of us will win. Wouldn't that be neat?"

Mataya smiled. "Yeah, but I doubt that I will. I hope you do, though."

"Come on, Taya. You have just as good of a chance to win as anyone else. You're a good writer."

Mataya shrugged. "But not good enough to win a contest. Besides, the winners get a new bike. And I have no use for a bike." She pointed at the metal braces on her legs and her crutches that leaned against the wall. "Why would I want to win something I can't even use?"

"I know there are some things you can't do, Taya. But

writing is something you *can* do. I think you should show people just how good of a writer you are." Shaylynne took her notebook out of her backpack. "Now, let's see. We need to decide what we're going to write about".

Mataya was thoughtful for a moment. "Well, we could write about our favorite hobbies or what we did last summer." She suggested.

"No, everyone will write about that stuff," Shaylynne replied.

Shaylynne's blue eyes danced with excitement. "Hey, I've got it! We could write about each other." Mataya looked at her, puzzled.

"Each other?"

Shaylynne nodded her head. "Sure, that would be fun. I'll write about you, and you write about me. We could write about being best friends."

"I don't know, Shay. I just don't think I–"

Shaylynne interrupted, "You can do it, Mataya. Give yourself a little more credit. At least give it a try. Please?"

Mataya sighed. "Well, Okay." Shay sounded so excited; she didn't feel like arguing with her. Instead, she reached over to pet Timber, and said, "He sure is a cool dog."

Shay agreed. "The best!"

2 - THE ESSAY CONTEST

*D*uring supper that evening, Mataya barely picked at her food.

"Mataya, is anything wrong? You've hardly touched your supper." Cherise Rhodes asked her daughter.

"Did something happen in school today?" Her father questioned.

"Mrs. Burke gave us a new assignment today. We have to write an essay for a contest. There will be one winner in each grade."

"That sounds like fun," Seth said. "What's the problem? You love to write."

"All the winners will have to read their essays at parents' night. "I can't get up on that stage and read in front of all those people."

"Well, just do your very best. I know you can win," Seth told his daughter.

"That's what Shay said too," Mataya said without much

enthusiasm. "She thinks we should write about each other, about being best friends."

"And I agree," Cherise said. "Shay is a very special friend. She should be easy to write about."

CHERISE QUIETLY ENTERED Mataya's bedroom later that night, checking to make sure she would be asleep.

"Mom?"

"Taya, what are you doing awake? It's after eleven."

"I can't sleep. Mom, do you and dad ever wish that I hadn't been born?" Mataya asked.

"Mataya Cherise Rhodes! Why would you even ask such a thing? Of course, we would never wish something like that."

"Well, sometimes, I do."

Cherise sat down on the edge of her daughter's bed. "Mataya, this isn't like you at all. "Are you still worried about reading in front of all those people?"

"I can't walk like the other k-kids. I can't run like they can. I can't even t-talk like they can. I can't ride a b-bike, so why s-should I try to win this contest?"

"It's not about winning the bike, honey. It's about showing your writing talent. Sure, you can't ride a bike, but there are so many things you can do."

"What do you mean?" Mataya asked.

"When you were first diagnosed with cerebral palsy, we were told that you would probably never walk, talk, or go to a traditional school, or do anything by yourself. But, you can walk, with braces and crutches. And you can do almost everything by yourself." Cherise took a breath, then continued. "You are a very determined little girl. There is no reason why you can't enter this contest. And you can win. We just ask that you give it your best shot."

Mataya yawned. "Ok, Mom. I'll try."

"That's my girl." Cherise leaned over and kissed her cheek. "Good night, hon."

"Night, Mom."

3 - THE ESSAY CONTEST

wo weeks later, Mataya was patiently sitting on a stool while her mother braided her hair to help get her ready for Shaylynne's thirteenth birthday party.

"Mom, do I have to go to this party?" Mataya asked with a sigh.

"Taya, Shay is your best friend. Of course, you have to go. Some of your other friends will be there too. Why wouldn't you want to go?"

"Because Shay's cousin Felicity will be there. And she doesn't like me." Mataya answered.

"Do you like her?" Cherise asked.

Mataya shook her head. "Not really."

"How come?" Her mom asked.

"I don't know. I guess because I know she doesn't like me." Cherise smiled.

"I think you and Felicity should make it a point to get to know each other better."

As Mataya walked over to Shaylynne's, she thought about what her mother had said. *Why should I try to be friends with Felicity? She doesn't like me.*

Before ringing the doorbell, she paused, took a deep breath, and thought, *Ok, I'll make an honest effort to be friends.*

"Hi, Taya." Shaylynne opened the door. "We're all in the living room." Mataya followed her best friend into the living room, where six other girls were seated on the floor.

"Hi Taya," was the greeting from the other girls, all seated in a circle on the floor.

Midnight was fast approaching as the girls settled themselves into their sleeping bags on the floor.

"Hey, have you guys finished your essay yet?" Kendra asked.

"Not yet," Norah answered. "Almost, though."

"I finished mine," Shaylynne answered. "How about you, Tay?"

Felicity chuckled softly. "She probably writes as slow as she talks."

Mataya was quiet for a moment." "Yeah, I finished mine," she said softly.

"Amazing." Felicity retorted.

"Felicity, those comments are totally unnecessary," Shaylynne told her cousin. "Why can't you be nice? Mataya has never done anything to you."

"Hey cousin, just because you want to be friends with a cripple doesn't mean that I have to be," Felicity answered loudly.

Mataya could feel her face turn red as tears burned her brown eyes. "I may be crippled, but I'm not deaf," Mataya whispered. "And anyway, I would rather be my kind of crippled than YOUR kind of crippled." She added after a brief pause. Felicity sat up and folded her arms across her chest.

"Excuse me? I'm not crippled. You don't see a brace on my legs, do you?"

"It's called ignorance. And that type of handicap is worse than any other." Felicity's face turned beet red as the other girls burst into laughter.

"She's got you there, Felicity," Shay told her cousin. Felicity grunted loudly as she settled back into her sleeping bag.

As Mataya settled down into her sleeping bag, she smiled to herself. *Maybe we can't be friends, but at least I stood up for myself.*

MATAYA GRADUALLY OPENED her eyes and glanced around the room. The other girls were still asleep, spread out in sleeping bags around the living room. Hearing sounds coming from the kitchen, she decided to get up.

She put on her braces as quietly as she could, trying not to bang them on the floor, then pulled herself to her feet with her crutches.

Mataya made her way to the kitchen. She found Shay's

dad Isaiah sitting at the table reading the paper, and her mother, Rebekah, was standing at the stove fixing breakfast.

"Good morning, Mataya," Isaiah said with a smile. "Did you sleep well?"

"Yes, I did. Thank you." Mataya answered politely. "The others are still asleep. Is it okay if I sit out here?"

"Of course, dear," Rebekah answered. "Shay told us about your essay assignment. That sounds exciting." Mataya shrugged.

"It's okay, I guess."

"You don't sound as excited as Shay is," Rebekah said. "For as long as I have known you, you have loved to write. You don't like the assignment?"

"Well, it's not that I don't like the assignment. I like the writing part. But all the winners get a bike." Mataya kicked one leg out to expose her brace. "I can't ride a bike, so I don't want to win. The bike should go to someone who can use it. Not someone who has to wear these stupid braces. If I can't use the prize, why try to win?" Mataya questioned, obvious frustration in her voice. Rebekah knelt in front of her and took her hands in her own.

"Honey, I do understand your frustrations in not being able to do some things that other children do. That's why it is so important that you do your best with things that you can do. You are a wonderful writer. It would be such an accomplishment. If you win the bike, you could always donate it to a needy child."

Mataya was quiet for a moment as she pondered her suggestion. *I guess I could do that, she thought to herself.*

Laughter from the living room announced that the other

girls were awake. Mataya pulled herself to her feet. "Sounds like everyone else is up. I'd better get in there." She headed towards the living room.

"Mataya, remember what I said," Rebekah said. Mataya nodded, then continued on her way.

"Ok, class. Here's the day you've been waiting for." Mrs. Burke stood in front of her sixth-grade class one week later on Friday afternoon. "I have the names of the winners of the essay contest. The ninth-grade winner is Sami Jo Michaels, the eighth-grade winner is Josh Abrahams, the seventh-grade winner is Kyle Travis, And the sixth-grade winner is our very own Mataya Rhodes."

"Alright, Taya!" Shaylynne patted her friend on the back. "I knew you could do it."

Mataya could only stare at her teacher in disbelief as some of her classmates broke into applause., while others, including Felicity, remained silent. In fact, Felicity was glaring at her.

"Congratulations, Mataya." Mrs. Burke smiled. "A job well done. Parent's night is two weeks from today. The winning essays will be read in the assembly that evening. You all did a tremendous job on your essays. You should all be very proud of yourself. I didn't know we had such—"

Mrs. Burke was interrupted by the 3:00 p.m. bell, announcing the end of the school day and beginning of the weekend. "Okay, class, you are dismissed. No homework. Have a good weekend, and I'll see you all on Monday."

The students wasted no time in gathering their books and racing for the door.

On the way out, Felicity pushed past Mataya and said, "They probably voted for you because you're a cripple!"

Mataya cringed and tried to think of a reply, but Felicity was already gone.

4 - THE ESSAY CONTEST

*C*herise was awakened by the ringing phone. She glanced at the clock on the nightstand beside the bed. *Who would be us calling at two in the morning?*

She reached over and picked it up. "Hello?" After a few seconds, she sat up and was fully awake. "What? Are they ok?" Cherise listened for a moment longer. "Oh, my Lord. Yes, I'll be right there."

Cherise hung up the phone, then shook her husband until he woke up. "Seth, I'm going to the hospital," she said before he had a chance to say anything. "Shay and her parents were in a car accident."

Hearing those words, Seth was wide awake. "What? How bad?"

"It doesn't sound good. I'll call you as soon as I can," Cherise replied as she quickly got dressed.

"Do you want me to go with you?" Seth asked, fully awake now. Cherise shook her head no.

"No, someone needs to stay with Mataya." Cherise kissed him quickly then hurried from the room.

CHERISE ARRIVED HOME several hours later. She found her husband sitting at the kitchen table. Seth put down the paper and stood to greet her. One look at her face told him the news wasn't good. A lump formed in his throat. "How bad?"

"Where's Mataya?" She asked softly.

"She's not up yet. Honey, please tell me."

Cherise wrapped her arms around his neck. As he held her, he could feel her whole body shake as she cried. After a few minutes, Cherise pulled away from him and hesitated as she searched for words.

"They were hit by a drunk driver. Shay…" Cherise paused as sobs overtook her, and she buried her face on his shoulder.

As he held her in his arms, his heart was heavy. "She didn't make it, did she?" He asked, barely above a whisper.

Cherise slowly shook her head. "No. She…she died at the scene."

Seth hugged her tighter as tears continued streaming down her cheeks. Shay was like a second daughter to them." As they tried to come to terms with the tragedy, neither of them heard their young daughter come into the kitchen

"Mom? Dad? What's going on? I got up to use the bathroom, and I heard you talking. Is something wrong?"

Cherise reluctantly pulled away from her husband and turned to face her.

Mataya looked at her Mom, then her Dad. She could tell that something was definitely not right.

Cherise glanced at Seth, then said softly, "Honey, come and sit down. There's something we have to tell you."

Mataya made her way over to the table, not taking her eyes off her parents.

Once she was seated, Cherise knelt in front of her and took her hands in her own. Seth stood beside his daughter, placing his hands on her shoulders.

"Honey, last night there was an accident––a bad accident. Uh…" Cherise searched for words.

"Who was it?" Mataya questioned, her tone scared. Cherise struggled for the words and finally took a deep breath. "It was Shay and her parents. They were—"

Mataya pulled away from her mom and jumped out of her chair. "No! Take me to her! She needs me to be with her. PLEASE!" Mataya picked up her crutches and started to head for the door.

Cherise looked at Seth, her eyes begging him to take over.

Seth reached over to Mataya and gently grabbed her arm. "Honey, the accident was bad, very bad. Shay—Shay didn't make it. She died at the scene."

Mataya stared at him in disbelief, shaking her head. "No. It can't be true. You're wrong. She can't be dead. I DON'T BELIEVE YOU!" Mataya pulled away from her father and headed towards her room as fast as her crutches would let her. Seconds later, they heard the bedroom door slam shut.

Seth turned and faced his wife. Cherise slowly shook her head. No words were necessary as their eyes said what they both were thinking, *what do we do? How do we comfort her?*

5 - THE ESSAY CONTEST

*I*n the days that followed, Mataya still couldn't believe that her best friend was gone. She refused to go to school, and her parents allowed her to stay home, as they understood the grief their daughter was feeling. They were both at a loss as to how to help her.

Mataya spent much of her time curled up on her bed with her curtains closed. Her bedroom window faced Shay's bedroom window, and she couldn't bear looking at it, knowing she wasn't there.

They had gone to her friend's funeral, which had been only a small gathering of family and friends. She hadn't been able to speak to Shay's parents. *What would she say to them?* She couldn't imagine their deep grief at the loss of their only child.

As Mataya lay there, lost in her own thoughts, she realized that tomorrow night was parent's night, and she was expected to get up in front of everyone to read her essay about her best friend. *I don't know if I can do this,* she thought.

Not without Shay. She looked upward toward the ceiling with fresh tears on her cheeks, she whispered softly, *"Shay, if you can hear me, please help me to know what to do. You encouraged me to write this essay, even though I didn't want to do it. I did my best, and I won. But winning means nothing to me. Not without you. I don't know if I can get up there tomorrow night and read it."* With those words, Mataya cried herself to sleep.

"HONEY, you don't have to do this," Cherise sat down on the bed beside her daughter. It was Parents Night, and Mataya was scheduled to read her winning essay. "Mrs. Burke will understand."

Mataya slowly shook her head. "I have to, Mom. For Shay." Mataya said, her voice quivering. "She wanted me to win. I couldn't have done it without her. I—-I" Mataya threw her arms around her mom and sobbed, her whole-body trembling. "I miss her so much." Her face buried on her mom's shoulder, her voice was muffled. "She was my very best friend. I need her, Mom."

Cherise gently rubbed her daughter's back as she held her. "I know, sweetheart. She was an amazing young girl. We were lucky to have her in our lives. She was family."

"I'm sorry to interrupt, but we need to get going," Seth said softly from the bedroom doorway.

Mataya pulled away from her mom and wiped her eyes with the back of her hands. She took a deep breath., and said, "I'm ready." She picked up her crutches and left the room, her parents following close behind.

"LADIES AND GENTLEMEN, our final essay tonight is a special one. The writer of this essay wrote about her best friend, Shaylynne Leighton. Earlier this week, Shaylynne was killed in a car accident. Mataya asked if she could read her essay as planned, as a tribute to her best friend."

Principal Bryce motioned for Mataya to come forward and announced, "Mataya Rhodes, our sixth-grade winner."

Mataya slowly approached the podium. Looking out at the large crowd, she wondered if maybe her mom had been right. *Maybe she shouldn't have come tonight?* The thought of reading out loud in front of so many people frightened her, as she remembered being teased because of her sometimes-slow speech. But then she thought about her friend and knew she had to do this for her.

She took a deep breath, then started to read slowly, occasionally stumbling on the words as her nerves threatened to take over.

"S-hay is my very best f-friend. We have been friends since k-kindergarten when s-she and her family moved in next door to us. She never teased me because I couldn't walk or run like she could, or b-because I talk slower than other kids. W-we like to do a lot of things together, like go to the zoo and the park. We both like to read and write. I like to write stories, and she likes to write poems."

Mataya stopped reading for a moment, not sure whether

or not she could finish. Finally, she took a breath and continued, her voice trembling.

"P-people say that I am special because I have c-cerebral palsy. But I think Shay is special because she cares about people. She doesn't do things that will hurt people's feelings. Shay is always the first to offer help to someone who needs it. She likes me even though I can't do a lot of things that she does. Shay always encourages me to try new things, even if I'm afraid of what others may think. I-I will never have another friend like Shay."

The audience, many with tears in their eyes, broke into thundering applause. Mataya made her way off the stage and into the waiting arms of her parents.

"Mataya?" Mataya turned at the sound of a soft voice behind her.

"Felicity." She quickly wiped the tears from her cheeks. "I need to go," she said quickly, afraid that Felicity would once again tease her for her slow speech.

Felicity reached out and touched her arm. "Please, Mataya. I want to talk to you. *Please?*"

Mataya shifted uneasily but nodded. "O-okay. What?"

Felicity lowered her gaze, then looked back up. "I want to say I'm sorry for teasing you. It was wrong of me. Your essay about Shay was beautiful. Really, it was. Shay always talked about you. I-I was jealous. I guess that's why I always teased you."

"Y-you were j-jealous...of me?" Mataya asked.

Felicity nodded. "Shay was my cousin. We were close. But you were her best friend. I wanted to be her best friend, not just her cousin. I resented your friendship with her." Felicity paused, lowering her gaze, then looked up again at Mataya as she continued. "Your essay showed me that I didn't need to be envious. Shay had enough love for all her friends. Even me. I know we can't be friends after the way I treated you, but I just wanted to say I'm sorry." Felicity turned and started walking away.

Mataya looked at her parents, then walked as fast as her crutches would allow, to catch up with Felicity. "Felicity, w-wait."

Felicity stopped and turned around.

"Who says we can't be friends?" Mataya questioned. "I think Shay w-would want us to be friends. Don't you?"

Felicity was quiet for a moment. "But after the way I treated you…" she replied, as her voice trailed off.

"Well, we can let that go, a-and start from today. That's what Shay would do, wouldn't she?"

Felicity nodded. Mataya was right. That's what her cousin would do. "Thank you, Mataya. For giving me another chance. Shay was lucky to have you for her best friend." With that, Felicity turned and disappeared into the crowd.

6 - THE ESSAY CONTEST

*M*ataya lay on her bed, thinking about how she and Shaylynne had been friends since kindergarten. From the first time they met, they had shared a very special friendship.

Tears streamed down her cheeks as sobs shook her entire body. I can't make it without you, Shay, she thought. Then, speaking in a whisper, she said, "You're my very best friend. Why did you have to leave me?"

A knock on the door brought Mataya back to the present. Without waiting for an answer, the door opened, and Cherise came in. "Honey, Shay's parents are here to see you."

"I can't see them, Mom. It hurts too much." Mataya said softly. Cherise nodded in understanding and left the room.

Seconds later, there was another knock on the door. Cherise and Seth came in, followed by Isaiah and Rebekah. Rebekah was holding Timberwolf, Shay's Yorkie puppy, that she had gotten last Christmas.

"Taya, your essay was beautiful," Rebekah said softly.

"You were there?" Taya asked, her voice barely above a whisper.

Rebekah nodded. "Yes. Shay was so excited that your essay had won. We wanted to go...for her."

"Mataya, we'd like you to have Timber," Isaiah said as he stepped forward. "This little guy was very important to Shay, and so were you. You've always been like a second daughter to us."

Mataya held the puppy gently in her arms. "Y-you're giving me Timberwolf? I-I don't understand."

Rebekah knelt down in front of her, speaking softly, and said, "Timber was Shay's pride and joy. But since the accident, he just hasn't been himself. He misses Shay too. He needs someone to love her and play with him. He needs you." Mataya hugged the puppy close to her.

"Y-you really want me to have him? Taya asked.

Rebekah gently touched Mataya's tear-stained cheek. "Yes, sweetheart. We really do. We wanted to give you something that meant something to our daughter, something that you could treasure, to remember her by. Nothing meant more to her than this puppy. And no friend was more special to her than you. We feel that Shay would want you to have him."

"I promise to take good care of him."

After they had gone, Mataya sat down at her desk, still holding the puppy in her arms. She picked up her winning essay that lay on her desk. She carefully folded the essay and placed it in her desk drawer.

Although she had lost her best friend, Shaylynne would be with her forever in her heart.

THE END

STORY TWO

The 'R' Word

AUTHOR'S NOTE

In this story, I used the words "retard" and "retarded." I used this word for one reason only—to educate people that the use of this word to describe a person with intellectual disabilities is hurtful, derogatory, and needs to be eradicated from the English language.

The "R" word is also often used in fun or to joke about things. For example, saying "I am such a retard" is just as wrong as using it about a person with disabilities. The "R" word is *not* a joke. There is nothing funny about this word.

Several years ago, Special Olympics started a campaign called "Spread the Word to End the Word." Please go to my blog page for a link to the site to take the pledge to not use this word.

https://www.alaskadp.com/rena-yeager-blog

1 - THE 'R' WORD

*H*eather Mackney opened the folder in front of her, then looked up at the two people sitting across from her, a young girl and her mother. "Thank you for coming in today, Mrs. Raddisson."

Jocelyne Raddisson shifted in her chair. "Is something wrong, Mrs. Mackney? Has Mariah done something wrong?"

Heather smiled. "Oh no, nothing like that. I just wanted to discuss something with you. And, I wanted Mariah to be here as this concerns her. The school year is almost over, and I wanted to talk to you about plans for next Fall. Mariah will be in eighth grade, and several of her teachers and I feel that she is a good candidate to be mainstreamed into a traditional school. We would like your thoughts. And Mariah's also."

14-year-old Mariah looked at her counselor, then at her mother. "Does this mean I won't be coming here anymore?"

Her mother nodded. "Yes, sweetheart. Now shush. Let's let Mrs. Mackney finish."

"Mariah has done excellent during her years here at Pine

Ridge. She has blossomed into a beautiful young lady. She has exceeded everyone's expectations. And her speech has improved greatly this past year. She hardly stutters at all now, unless she's nervous. We feel she will do well in a traditional school with non-disabled children."

Jocelyne was silent for a moment as she thought about what the counselor had just told her. Although pleased that her daughter had done so well, she wasn't sure she was ready to be moved out of the school she had been in since kindergarten. "Pine Ridge has been her safe haven since she was five years old. Going to a traditional school—wow, I'm not sure she is ready. It's such a big step."

Mrs. Mackney nodded. "Yes, it is. But this is what we prepare our students for. Some go through their entire school experience here. And others graduate to mainstreaming into traditional schools." Mrs. Mackney paused briefly, then continued. "Mariah is ready. She deserves this opportunity. But the decision is yours and Mariah's. If you feel she isn't ready, or if she doesn't want to make the switch, she, of course, will be welcome to remain here at Pine Ridge."

"I'm going to need to think about this and discuss it with Mariah," she said, as she looked over to her daughter.

Mrs. Mackney smiled. "Take as much time as you need. It is a big decision and not one to be made hastily. If you have any questions, feel free to give me a call."

Jocelyne and her daughter stood to leave. "I will, Mrs. Mackney. Thank you."

"I will be looking forward to hearing from you."

"Mom, d-do I have to do this?" Mariah asked.

Jocelyne pulled the car out of the school parking lot. "No, sweetheart, not if you don't want to. But I think we need to talk about it. Your teachers feel you are ready."

Mariah shook her head. "N-no. I-I'm not...ready. A-all my friends a-are at Pine Ridge." Mariah folded her arms across her chest, an action her mother had learned years ago that could turn into a battle of wills.

"Now Mariah, don't go giving me that attitude of yours. Nothing has been decided yet. We will discuss it and come to a decision together. I realize Pine Ridge is your safety zone, and all your friends are there. But you need to realize what an opportunity this is. Many children with disabilities spend all their school years in schools for people with disabilities. They may never get a chance to grow by attending a traditional school."

"I-I don't want to go," Mariah replied with defiance in her voice.

"We'll talk about it," Jocelyne said in a tone that told Mariah this was the end of the discussion, at least for now. The rest of the ride home was silent as they were each lost in their own thoughts concerning the situation at hand.

"I'M GOING t-to take Prince for a walk," Mariah said upon arriving home, referring to her German Shepherd. It was her job to walk him each afternoon. She put his leash on, and the large dog walked beside her as they made their way outside.

"M-Mom wants me to go t-to a traditional school,"

Mariah said, her stuttering increasing as she got more nervous thinking about it. They walked towards the end of their block. "B-but, I-I don't...I don't want to go."

Prince whined as if he understood what she had said.

Mariah knelt down and put her arms around his neck. "Y-you un–understand, d-don't you, boy? You are my best friend in the w-whole world. I c-can't talk to Mom. I–I wish Daddy was here. He wouldn't m-make me go to that school." Tears welled up in her eyes as she thought about her father, who had died a year earlier in a tragic car accident.

They had reached the end of their block. Mariah sat down on the nearby bench, Prince lay down at her feet. Mariah thought about the conversation that had taken place in Mrs. Mackney's office. She slowly shook her head. *I won't go,* she thought with determination.

"Hi, Mariah."

Mariah glanced up to see two boys her own age on bicycles. She knew one of them as her neighbor, but the other boy she hadn't seen before. "H-Hi, Brennan."

Brennan reached down to pet Prince. "Hi-ya Prince."

Mariah saw the strange boy staring down at her legs. Oh, how she wished she could hide her metal leg braces. "W-who is that?" Mariah asked, pointing at the other boy.

"This is Tad. Tad, this is my neighbor Mariah and her dog Prince."

Tad snickered. "Let's go, Brennan. We don't have time to hang out with this retard."

Brennan was surprised and not sure how to respond. He looked at Mariah, embarrassed.

Not getting the reaction he expected, Tad continued,

"Well, it's what she is. Look at her. She wears braces and can't even talk right."

Mariah hung her head as she got up to leave. "Come-come on, Prince." She gave a gentle tug on his leash.

After she had gone, Brennan turned to face his friend. "Why did you do that?"

Tad laughed. "Because it's fun. She's probably used to it. Come on, let's go."

Before Brennan could say anything else, Tad turned his bike around and headed down the street.

He turned his bike around and followed. Maybe he could talk to him later about it. He and Tad had a lot in common, and he liked having him for a friend.

2 - THE 'R' WORD

*J*ocelyne took a sip of her coffee as she thought about the conversation with Heather Mackney. She was torn as to what might be best for her daughter.

Oh, Aiden. What should I do? She sighed heavily. She missed her husband so much. He would know what to do.

As she sat alone at the kitchen table, her thoughts drifted back to a night 14 years earlier…

It was Valentine's Day, and in the middle of a romantic celebration, they had welcomed a beautiful baby girl. The perfect baby they had long waited for.

As she held her new baby in her arms, she gushed over her like all new mothers do, counting her fingers and her toes. Her beautiful eyes made her smile. Little did her parents know that these eyes held a secret, a secret that would dictate the direction their lives would take.

A few hours after the birth of their first child, she and Aiden had been discussing a name for their daughter. They had chosen not to find out in advance the sex of their baby.

After much discussion, they had finally agreed on Mariah, after Aiden's Grandmother, and Grace after her Grandmother. They had just settled on her name when Dr. Pachey came in.

Jocelyne had started to excitedly tell her that their new daughter had a name but stopped when she saw the grim look on Dr. Pachey's face. "What is it? Is something wrong with our daughter?" She reached over and gripped her husband's hand.

Dr. Pachey pulled up a chair and sat down. She was silent for a moment as she stared into their waiting faces. She took a deep breath. "I'm glad you're here, Aidan. I need to discuss something with you both." Dr. Pachey cleared her throat. "I suspected right away that your daughter could have Down Syndrome. Upon a physical exam and a blood test called a Karyotype, my initial diagnosis is correct. I'm sorry."

The parents were silent for a moment as they tried to grasp this news. Aiden was the first to speak. "Down Syndrome? What exactly is this? How can you tell in a newborn? She looks perfectly normal to us."

"A child born with Down Syndrome has several facial features such as small head and ears, bulging tongue, eyes that slant upwards, broad short hands with a single crease in the palm, tiny white spots on the colored part of the eye, called Brushfields Spots. She--"

Aiden quickly interrupted. "If you suspected our baby has this—has this Down Syndrome, why didn't you tell us? How could we not have known something was wrong?"

"I wanted to do the blood test to make sure. There is no doubt now that your daughter has Down Syndrome. Unless you are familiar with this, you wouldn't know what to look for, the facial features, and the single crease on her palms."

Jocelyne had been silently taking the information in. She looked up at Dr. Pachey and said softly. "What does this mean for her when she grows up?"

"Down Syndrome causes physical and developmental delays and disabilities. Children with Downs may not walk or talk until older. Some never walk or talk. They learn slower than other children. They—"

Aiden interrupted again, "You mean our baby is retarded?"

Dr. Pachey shook her head. "Yes, that is what these children were called years ago, but we prefer not to use that word. Now, we use the term intellectually disabled."

"Is Down Syndrome hereditary?" Jocelyne asked. "I mean, what caused it? Did I do something while I was pregnant?"

Dr. Pachey lightly touched her arm. "No, no. It was nothing you did. Downs is not hereditary. It is a genetic disorder caused when abnormal cell division results in an extra full or partial copy of chromosome 21, which is why this is often referred to as Trisomy 21. The extra genetic material causes the developmental changes and physical features of Down Syndrome."

Jocelyne laid back against her pillow and closed her now

teary eyes. Aiden was silent as he put his arms around her, fighting back his own tears.

Dr. Pachey stood up to leave. "I'm going to leave you two alone now. Call if you need anything or have further questions."

⚜

THE SLAMMING door jolted Jocelyne back to the present. Prince ran into the kitchen with Mariah close behind.

"How was your walk," she asked her daughter.

Mariah only shrugged, then excused herself and made her way down the hall to her bedroom.

Mariah usually returned from her walks full of laughter and chatter. *That was strange. Something must have happened*, she thought to herself as she headed down to her daughter's room.

She lightly knocked on the door. "Mariah, honey? Can I come in?" When she received no answer, she gently opened the door. She found her daughter sitting on the window seat, staring outside, with her braces off, and her arms wrapped around her knees.

"Did something happen while you were on your walk?" Jocelyne patiently waited for her daughter to answer.

After a few moments of silence, Mariah turned to look at her mother, crying. "Mom, why do-why do kids u–use that word?"

Jocelyne looked at her puzzled, then sat down beside her. "Honey, maybe you should tell me what happened."

Mariah told her mother about meeting Brennan and Tad and that Tad had called her a retard. "Why, Mom?"

Jocelyne shook her head. "I don't know, sweetheart. Some people just don't understand how much that word hurts others. They think of it as a joke."

"But-but it's n–not funny. It h–hurts."

Tears welled up in Jocelyne's eyes, seeing the hurt in her daughter's almond-shaped eyes. What could she say to take away her pain? *Kids could be so cruel sometimes,* she thought. *Will sending her to a traditional school be a good idea? Am I opening up a world of hurt for my daughter? A world where she will be teased?* Now unsure, she sighed. School was almost out for the summer, so she had time to think about it, to make sure she was making the best possible decision for her daughter.

3 - THE 'R' WORD

*T*he next three weeks passed quickly, and all too soon, it was the last day of school, and it found Jocelyne and Mariah back in the Counselor's office discussing plans for the upcoming school year.

"I just wanted to touch base with you regarding the next school year," the counselor Mrs. Mackney said.

Jocelyne sighed. "I'm glad you feel Mariah would do well in a traditional school, and I have been considering this for the past few weeks. I have gone back and forth between staying here at Pine Ridge or moving her to a new school. I had decided that moving her would be good, but now I'm not so sure. Something happened a few weeks ago that makes me wonder if moving her would be a mistake."

Mrs. Mackney walked around the desk and sat on the corner, raising her eyebrows in a question.

Mariah shifted uneasily in her chair, then spoke softly. "H–he called-he called me a retard."

"What? Mariah, who called you this?"

Mariah shrugged. "A–a friend of Brennan's. H–he was *mean.*" The last word was barely above a whisper.

"Mrs. Mackney, I'm not sure that sending her to the other school will be best. Here, she has friends, she isn't teased, people don't call her that ugly word. She's happy here." Jocelyne continued. "I don't want to send her someplace where there will be nothing but hurt."

"I'm sorry this happened. We want to do what's best for them. But that isn't realistic. At some point, they need to be out in the world, away from protective walls." Mrs. Mackney took a breath, then continued. "Our kids need to educate others about this word and why it isn't ok. They need to teach people about their need to belong, to show others what this word means, show them why this word is *NEVER* acceptable." Mrs. Mackney smiled at Mariah. "I believe Mariah is capable of doing this. Please give this matter more consideration. The two of you talk it over, and we will touch base again later this summer."

Jocelyne glanced at her daughter. "How about it, sweetheart? Can we think about it a little longer?"

Mariah nodded. "Y-yes. I-I guess so. But I c-can come back here…if I want?"

Heather nodded. "Yes, but I want you to seriously consider this move, Mariah. It will help you someday to live on your own. Do we have a deal?"

Mariah nodded hesitantly.

Mrs. Mackney smiled. "Great. Then I will see you later this summer."

Jocelyne and Mariah stood to leave. "Thank you, Mrs. Mackney. We'll keep in touch."

4 - THE 'R' WORD

*M*ariah always looked forward to the last day of school because it meant that her yearly trip to Camp Bridge was only a few weeks away. For the two weeks leading up to camp, she was busy packing, shopping, and making sure she had everything she would need.

Finally, the big day had arrived, and Mariah and her mother were on their way to Camp Bridge, a two-hour drive from their home.

"So, honey, have you given any more thought to switching schools?" Jocelyne asked once they were on their way.

Mariah was silent for a moment, staring out the window. After a brief silence, she answered slowly. "W-what if the kids...make fun of me? What...what if they...call me that.... that name. The 'R' word?"

Jocelyne sighed. "Honey, I know some kids can be mean. They don't know how much it hurts when they call someone that word. They aren't taught that it hurts."

"Why…. doesn't…. doesn't someone teach them?"

"Well, sometimes the adults don't realize it either. They are ignorant; they don't understand. "

"Someone…someone should teach them," Mariah said softly

"Mariah, I think you should try the new school. Just maybe for a couple of months, see how it goes. Mrs. Mackney said you could go back to Pine Ridge if you don't like it. How about trying it just until…. let's say just until Christmas."

Mariah was thoughtful for a moment, then turned to her mother. "Let…let me think about it. I…will let…. let you know…. after… after camp."

Jocelyne nodded. "Fair enough."

Mother and daughter continued the drive in silence, each lost in their own thoughts.

ALL TOO SOON, the week at camp came to an end. Mariah was sitting on the bench outside her cabin while waiting for her mother. She sat beside a new camp friend, Morgan. The two girls had been cabinmates this week.

"Do you go to a traditional school or a special school?" Morgan asked.

"I go to a special school. B-but they want me t-to move to a traditional school. But I-I don't want to."

"How come?" Morgan asked.

"I don't want to be t-teased. Or c-called the 'R' word."

"That's how I felt when I got moved, but now I love my new school."

"Did they…tease you?" Mariah questioned.

Morgan nodded. "At first they did. They called me things like stupid, slow, cripple, and the 'R' word, and it really hurt. I wanted to go back to my old school. But my parents wanted me to stay and give it a chance. They said people don't understand how the 'R' word can hurt."

Mariah nodded. "That's what m-my Mom said. She said they need to be t-taught. She w-wants me to try it out… till Christmas."

"Are you going?" Mariah shrugged.

"I-I don't know. I like my school. I have f-friends there."

"You will make new friends. I think you should give it a try. Maybe you could teach the kids at the new school about the 'R' word.

Mariah was thoughtful for a moment. "Yeah, maybe. I guess. I could give it a t-try."

Morgan stood up. "Here come my folks. Good luck, Mariah. See you next summer."

Mariah nodded as she said goodbye to her new friend.

5 - THE 'R' WORD

The rest of the summer flew by, and soon it was the first day of school. Jocelyne had been pleased when her daughter had told her she had decided to give the new school a try.

Both were nervous as the day approached. Jocelyne didn't want to see her daughter get hurt but felt this was best for her, to allow her to grow and learn to live in a world with disabled and non-disabled people.

Later that morning, Jocelyne pulled up in front of the school. She opened her door, but Mariah stopped her.

"I-I…. want to go… alone. I don't… want them t-to think I am a-a baby."

Jocelyne forced a smile. "Okay, sweetheart. You can do this. I will pick you up right here at three."

Mariah nodded, then slowly got out of the car. She stood on the sidewalk until her mom drove away, then she slowly made her way to the entrance of the school, fully aware of the stares from other children as she passed.

Jocelyne pulled over to the curb a short distance away, then glanced in the rearview mirror, watching as her daughter walked alone into the school. She was nervous about this new change, probably more so than her daughter. As hard as it was, she had to allow Mariah to do things on her own. This was a big step for both of them.

"GOOD MORNING, EVERYONE," Stella Manning said, greeting her class of eighth-grade students. "I would like to introduce you to our new student, Mariah Raddisson. I'm trusting all of you to make her feel welcome."

Mariah glanced nervously around the room. She felt a sense of relief when she saw Brennan. But then noticed his friend Tad sitting in the desk behind him.

"Mariah, you may take the seat over there, in the front row." Mrs. Manning pointed to a seat beside a blonde hair girl. Mariah nodded as she made her way to the desk and sat down.

The girl beside her leaned over and whispered, "Hi. My name is Holliebeth."

Before Mariah could answer, she heard a voice behind her.

"Hey, look, it's the retard."

Mariah lowered her gaze, fighting the tears that threatened to spill down her cheeks.

"Tad, that is not called for. One more crack like that, and you will be sent to the principal's office. Do you understand me?" Mrs. Manning said firmly.

Tad shrunk down in his seat. "Yes, Mrs. Manning."

"Now welcome back, everyone. I trust that you all had a good summer vacation. I know you're probably all thinking it went by too quickly, but like they say, all good things must come to an end. I think we will have a good year together.

Mariah carefully glanced around the room. She wasn't so sure she wanted to stay here. She missed her old school, her friends. She had already been called that dreaded word once, and she hoped that it would be the last. After lunch, she followed her new classmates outside. She sat down on a nearby bench.

"Hey retard, wanna play kickball?" Tad shouted from a short distance away, then burst out laughing.

"Shut up, Tad, or I'm telling Mrs. Manning," Holliebeth yelled back as she sat down beside Mariah. "Don't pay any attention to him. He is such a jerk." Holliebeth rolled her eyes. Her gaze dropped down to the metal braces on Mariah's legs.

"How come you wear those braces?"

"T-they help k-keep my legs straight," Mariah answered. "And the...they help s-strengthen my l-legs."

Soon the bell rang, and the break was over. Holliebeth and Mariah, who walked much slower due to her braces, brought up the back of the line into the classroom.

"How was your first day?" Jocelyne asked later that afternoon when Mariah got into the car.

"I h-hate it. I want to go back to Pine Ridge," Mariah said firmly.

"What happened?" Jocelyne asked her daughter.

Mariah told her mother about Tad and his friends. Jocelyne shook her head. "I'm sorry that happened, honey. But it was only the first day. It will get better. I promise."

Mariah shook her head. "I'm n-not going back."

"I'm sorry, Mariah. But you need to give it more of a chance. We agreed to try it until Christmas. Then if you still feel this way, you can go back to Pine Ridge."

"But t-they don't l-like me. "Mariah argued.

"They don't Know you, Mariah. Once they get to know you, you will have lots of friends. Did you meet any other kids?"

"I sit next to a girl. Her n-name is H-Holliebeth. She seems nice."

Jocelyne smiled. "That's wonderful, honey. Maybe she will be your first friend at your new school."

Mariah shrugged. "M-maybe."

6 - THE 'R' WORD

*O*ver the next couple of weeks, Holliebeth and Mariah had become friends. *Maybe staying here won't be so bad,* Mariah thought to herself, *now that I have a friend.*

Tad's teasing continued. Not in the classroom, but out on the schoolyard. He didn't care if Holliebeth heard, but he did lay off when Brennan was around.

Holliebeth could see the hurt in her friend's eyes each time Tad called her a retard or imitated her stuttering. "Don't pay any attention to him, Mariah, he's a jerk. I've known Tad since kindergarten; he's always been this way. So it's not just you he teases."

Mariah looked up at her friend, with tears in her eyes. "B–but the 'R' word h-hurts."

"The 'R' word?" Holliebeth asked. "Why do you call it that?"

"T-they taught us at my other school…not to say R-retarded o-or retard. Just the 'R' word."

Holliebeth shrugged. "It's just a word, Mariah."

Mariah shook her head. "It hurts. People u-use it to talk about people with d-disabilities, like me. They use it to talk about people...like me...who are slow. Or people who don't learn as quickly as others. I am a person...just like everyone e-else."

"How come you hardly stutter when you're talking to me?"

"Because...I feel more comfortable around you," Mariah replied. "You're...my friend." Mariah tried to smile as she looked at her.

Holliebeth was thoughtful for a moment as she considered what Mariah had said. She herself had sometimes used the 'R' word in fun, but that was before she had met Mariah. In fact, a few of her classmates used it as an insult, often when they were joking around. But now, she realized it had deeply hurt her friend. Right then, she vowed to herself never to use the word again. Suddenly, a thought occurred to her. "I'll be right back."

Before Mariah could say anything, her friend turned and ran into the school.

"OKAY, CLASS, TAKE YOUR SEATS." Mrs. Manning stood by the door of the classroom as the students came in from recess. Once they were all seated, she walked to the front of the room.

"This afternoon, we are going to do something a little different. Instead of our usual spelling test, I want each of you to write a short essay about yourself. It should be about what you want others to know about you." She glanced at the clock. "I will give you one hour. Then, in the last part of the afternoon, we will read our essays out loud."

Mariah leaned over and whispered to Holliebeth. "I don't know what to write."

Holliebeth smiled. "Write about what you told me outside about the "R" word. I told Mrs. Manning about it, and she agreed that we need to make people aware of how the word hurts and shouldn't be used."

Mariah nodded as she picked up her pencil and started writing.

As the children busied themselves working on their essays, Mrs. Manning walked around the room, looking at the progress of the assignment.

"Ok, class, time is up." Mrs. Manning announced when the hour was up. "So who would like to read their essay first. If no one volunteers, I will pick someone."

No one volunteered.

"Okay, then. Brennan, come on up." Mrs. Manning said.

Brennan walked to the front of the room and began reading his essay.

Mariah squirmed in her seat, knowing that soon it would be her turn. She leaned over and whispered something to Holliebeth, who nodded. After Brennan had finished reading, Holliebeth raised her hand.

Mrs. Manning nodded at her. "Yes, Holliebeth? Would you like to go next.?"

Holliebeth walked to the front and whispered to Mrs.

Manning. "Mariah asked me to read for her. Her stutter gets worse when she is nervous."

"I see." She turned back to face the students. "Holliebeth will be reading for Mariah."

"Okay, then. Go ahead."

Holliebeth went back to Mariah's desk and picked up her paper. As she walked back to the front of the room, several students were looking at Mariah. Mrs. Manning nodded at her, indicating she could start reading.

Holliebeth cleared her throat, then started reading...

"My name is Mariah Raddisson. I am 14 years old. I was born with Down Syndrome. Down Syndrome is a condition in which a child is born with an extra copy of their twenty-first chromosome. You can't catch Down Syndrome. This makes me learn slower than other kids. I learn differently than you. People call me retarded or retard. People use it as a joke. Or to talk about people who are disabled or slow. This word is not funny. This word hurts. I am a person. I am not the 'R' word. I like the same things as you. I need the same things as you. I can learn the same things as you, just in my own way. I stutter. People tease me a lot. People call me stupid. But I am not."

Holliebeth paused as she looked at Mariah, who was looking down at her desk. She continued...

"They don't understand how this word hurts people. People need to be kind to people who are different. Please don't call people the "R" word. They need friends, just like you do. They are people just like you. The next time you want to call someone the "R" word, stop

*and think about how you would feel if someone called you that. I
am glad I came here, but sometimes it's hard. I just wanted you to
know that."*

Holliebeth folded the paper and went back to her seat.
She saw several students who were now looking at Mariah,
nodding their understanding, and appreciating how difficult
it must have been to write that. Shelly, being one of them,
whispered to Mariah, "Good job!"

Tad sat there stone-faced, staring straight ahead.

"Thank you, Mariah, for sharing, and Holliebeth for reading. Let's see who's next." Mrs. Manning looked down at her
class list, and then around the room. She pointed and said,
"Tad, you will be next."

Tad groaned as he stood up and made his way to the front
of the classroom. He read slowly and stumbled over several
of the words. As he went back to his desk, he heard some
snickering, and someone whispered, *"retard."* He looked over
to see who it was but only saw more of them snickering,
looking down at their desks, trying not to be noticed by Mrs.
Manning. As he sat down, embarrassed, he glared at his
essay, now laying on his desk in front of him.

Mrs. Manning frowned and said, "That will be enough
people. Not everyone can read as well as others."

Tad had just looked up at her as she had said it. Red-
faced, knowing she was talking about him, he looked down
and scratched out the words of his essay.

Mrs. Manning looked at the clock, and said, "Okay, class, ,
we'll continue after the lunch break is over." The bell rang,
and the students filed out of the room towards the cafeteria.

7 - THE 'R' WORD

*H*ey, Brennan! Wait up!" Tad hurried into the cafeteria to catch up with his friend. Brennan stopped to wait for him. They went through the food line with their trays and found a seat at an empty table.

While they ate, Tad was thinking of the classroom jokes made at his expense. Trying to shake off his own stumbling essay performance, he said, "Wasn't Mariah's essay lame?" He said as he finished his glass of milk.

"Why do you say that?" Brennan asked, taking a bite. He was looking down at his food, not wanting to hear Tad tease Mariah, and trying to think of a different subject.

"Well, you know, this 'R' word stuff. I don't see what the big deal is. She's just a big baby. She can't take it." Tad said with a snicker. "And I think she should have had to read her own essay."

"She has a hard time talking in front of people."

"That's the point. We could have h-h-heard h-h-her st-st-

stutter," Tad said, doing his best Mariah stuttering impression, and now had a big grin on his face.

Brennan, not smiling, looked up and noticed Mariah, who Tad had not seen, sit down at the table behind him. Holliebeth was on the way over, carrying glasses of juice for herself and Mariah. Mariah had a hard time trying to carry a tray of food and a beverage at the same time. The hurt in Mariah's eyes was unmistakable. The first time he had introduced him to Mariah, Tad had called her retarded. Brennan hadn't liked it then but hadn't said anything, and now felt bad about it. Best friend or not, he decided to tell him what he thought, even though sticking up for Mariah could jeopardize that. But he knew in his heart that this would be the right thing to do. "Tad, you need to stop!" Brennan said loud enough for others to hear.

"Stop what?" Tad asked, folding his arms across his chest.

They had both gotten up, getting ready to head outside for the after-lunch break.

"You know what. Stop teasing Mariah. She has never done anything to you. It wasn't easy for her to leave her other school to come here."

"Then maybe she should go back to her retard school," Tad said, dripping with sarcasm.

Brennan had enough. "I said knock it off!" he said as he gave Tad a hard push. Tad hit the floor and looked up at him with surprise on his face. Brennan pointed at him and continued, "I don't like the way you treat Mariah. Find yourself a new friend." With that, Brennan stormed outside to the schoolyard, oblivious to the crowd of students that had been witness to his kerfuffle with Tad. Outside, he sat down on a nearby bench.

As Tad lay there, too shocked to get up yet, a couple of his classmates were walking past, looking down at him, and shaking their head. Shelly glared at him and said, "Hey Tad, the way you bumbled your essay, I'd say you're the one who sounds retarded." She stepped over his leg as she walked by.

Shawn, walking beside her, said, "Yeah, who are you to talk. *Retard!*"

More students passed him on their way out and snickered. *"Serves him right...what a creep,"* another one said just loud enough for him to hear.

Holliebeth passed him and glared. Mariah looked at him sadly as she carefully made her way by him.

Now he realized what Brennan had said was true...the word was hurtful. He thought of when he heard it whispered after his essay. He felt humiliated.

With his face still red, Tad walked outside to the playground and looked for Brennan. Seeing him on the bench, he went and sat down beside him. Brennan had his arms crossed and was looking down at the ground, ignoring him.

For a moment, neither of them spoke.

Tad cleared his throat. "Brennan, I've been thinking. We've been best friends for a long time. I don't want a new best friend. I thought about retard..." Tad stopped and corrected himself. "The 'R' word. You're right. It didn't sound so good when people were calling me that. I guess Mariah doesn't deserve it either." Now, Tad was looking down at the ground. "Well, I...I guess no one does. Will you be my friend again if I stop teasing her?"

Brennan stared at him for a moment, looking for sincerity. Satisfied that his friend meant what he was saying, he nodded. "On one condition."

"What's that?" Tad asked, afraid of what he would say.

"You have to apologize to Mariah," Brennan told him.

Tad gave a sigh of relief. "I can do that," he said quietly. The bell rang, and both boys stood and went back into the school.

THE ESSAYS WERE FINISHED moments before the final bell of the day rang. Mariah was gathering her books while Holliebeth waited for her.

"Mariah?"

Mariah turned around to see Tad standing behind her, and grimaced.

Before Mariah could say anything, Holliebeth glared at him and said, "What do you want, Tad?"

Tad's face was red. "I want to apologize," he said, looking directly at Mariah. "I've treated you rotten since the first time I saw you that day walking your dog. I don't read very good...well, you heard my essay. So, I was talking to Brennan, trying to be cool, and making fun of you...he...well, you heard that too, and saw what happened." He paused for a breath, and continued, "Your essay was really good. I promise I won't call you the "R" word ever again."

Mariah, surprised, but pleased, replied, "T-thank you, Tad."

Holliebeth shook her head, surprised as Mariah was. "Are

you serious, Tad? I've never heard you apologize before. Why should we believe you?"

"Yeah, I know, but after making a fool of myself, pretty much in front of everybody, and almost losing my best friend over it, I guess I wised up. I really am sorry. To you, too, Holliebeth." He looked down, not sure what to do next.

Holliebeth looked at Mariah. "Well, what do you think, should we forgive him?

Mariah smiled. She knew that it hadn't been her essay that had changed his heart. It had been the kerfuffle between Brennan and him, and the threat of losing his best friend. But she didn't care what had caused the change; she was glad. "I think so. That means...that means a lot, Tad."

"Well, okay. So, I'll see you two around?" They nodded, so he turned and headed out the door, relieved. It felt strange to apologize but good. He went to look for Brennan. Time to apologize to him too.

Mariah and Holliebeth left the classroom. Once outside, Holliebeth said, "Well, that was new. How are you doing?"

Mariah gave her a big smile. "Much better. I think I'll stay. See you tomorrow?"

Mariah walked as fast as her braces would allow when she saw her Mother's car. As she got in, she thought, *Mrs. Mackney, my friend Morgan at camp, and Mom have been right. People need to be educated on the impact the "R" word has.* She hadn't wanted to leave her old school to move to this one but now was glad. After all, she had taught a bunch of people about the "R" word. And now she was anxious to tell others.

THE END

STORY THREE

Sofie's Christmas Miracle

1 - SOFIE'S CHRISTMAS MIRACLE

*I*t was Christmas again, and 14-year-old Sofie stared out the window of the bedroom she shared with five other girls. Her three years in the Children's Home had taught her only one thing––people don't care about older children; they only care about babies.

With a heavy sigh, Sofie turned away from the window and sat down on the edge of her bed. She glanced around the room. Decorations covered the walls.

"Hey, Sofie, we're gonna decorate the tree! Come and help!"

Sofie turned to see six-year-old Kerisa standing in the doorway, her eyes shining with anticipation of the Christmas holiday.

"I'll pass," Sofie answered.

The little girl persisted. "Awww, come on, Sofie. Please? It will be fun."

"I said no, Kerisa. Leave me alone." As soon as the words were out, Sofie regretted them. She could see the hurt in the younger girl's blue eyes. Her tone softened. "I'm sorry. I just don't want to right now. Maybe later."

Without another word, Kerisa turned and ran from the room. Sofie sighed heavily - she was like that at her age. But that seemed so very long ago, and things were different now.

Why did things have to change? Why did her mother have to leave her? These same questions had haunted her for three years. Questions that she had never found the answers for.

For the first eleven years of her life, it had just been her and her mom. They had been close, best friends, really. Her father had never been in her life, as he had left her mother before she had been born. Her mother seldom spoke of him, and she had learned at an early age to not ask questions about him.

"I THOUGHT I might find you here."

Sofie turned at the sudden voice. "Oh, hi, Dianna. What are you doing here?"

Dianna Wellington sat down on the bed beside her. "Just stopping by to see how you're doing. How come you're not down decorating the tree with everyone else?"

Sofie shrugged but remained silent.

"Honey, I know Christmas is a difficult time for you," Dianna continued. "I wish there was something I could do to help make it easier. I know—"

"You can't bring my mom back," Sofie said, interrupting her case manager.

"No, I can't," Dianne answered. "But I would like to find a

way to ease your pain some, help you to enjoy Christmas, start living again."

Sofie was silent for a moment, then turned to face Dianna. "Are you serious, Dianna? My mom is dead, and you want me to enjoy Christmas? She died right before Christmas. I hate Christmas! And nothing you say is ever going to change that! Now please just go away and leave me alone!"

"Sofie—"

"I said, leave me alone!" Sofie ran from the room, slamming the door behind her.

In her 20 years as a case manager, Dianna had worked with children of all ages. She had encountered children with behavior issues, anger issues, and many other problems.

But for some reason unknown to her, Sofie was different. Something about her just melted Dianna's heart, and she wanted to go the extra mile to make the child happier. She knew the tragedy of her mother's death would always be with her, but she wanted to help her move forward.

Dianna sighed heavily and thought, there must be something I can do to help her. But what?

DIANNA LEANED back in her chair. She just couldn't get young Sofie off her mind.

"Hey, Dianna, you look deep in thought. Something on your mind?" Jerrod McNeil asked as he sat down on the edge of her desk, waiting for her to answer.

Dianna was silent for a moment, a thoughtful expression on her face. She glanced up at her co-worker. "Jerrod, let me ask you something. I've got a 14-year-old girl whose mom died in a car accident three years ago, shortly before Christmas. Her father has never been in her life, and there are no known relatives, so for the past three years, she has been living at Kiddy Corners Children's Home. Because her mom died around the holidays, she hates Christmas. I need to figure out a way to get her involved in holiday activities, decorating, etc. She is angry, withdrawn, and just so sad. I want to know how to help her."

"Wow, that's a tough one," Jerrod replied. "Losing a parent at any time is rough, but during the holidays?"

"Any suggestions?" Dianna questioned When Jerrod didn't answer, Dianna continued. "She is the oldest child there. She is convinced that people only want to adopt babies and younger children."

"The sad thing is, she is probably right," Jerrod said with a sigh. "I wish I had a solution. It's hard for the older children to watch the younger ones get adopted."

"Even if I could place her in a foster home, at least she would be with a family. But none of our foster homes have openings right now. Sofie is such a sweet girl. Any family would love to have her. If they could just see beyond her age. How can we get people to consider taking an older child? It's just so unfair."

"I know what you mean, Dianna. Sounds to me like you are breaking our first rule...getting emotionally attached to one of our children."

"How can I not?" Dianna retorted. "These children don't deserve a life in the system. They deserve loving families. I have been Sofie's case manager for three years. I felt she needed extra attention after she lost her mother and suffered her own injuries. I took her for her surgeries and took her to all her PT sessions. I sort of bonded with her.

Jerrod shook his head. "I'm just sayin' that you shouldn't get too attached. You know that.

"Well, I need to find a way to help her to like life again," Dianna said. "Maybe even to enjoy Christmas again."

"Does she ever talk about her Mom? Jerrod asked.

Dianna shook her head. "No. Whenever I bring her up, she shuts down."

"Poor kid. I can't even imagine how she must feel."

Dianna glanced at her watch. "I've got an appointment. If you come up with any suggestions, let me know. Christmas is only three weeks away. I would like to make this Christmas special for her."

Jerrod nodded. "I'll see what I can come up with. Talk to you later."

2 - SOFIE'S CHRISTMAS MIRACLE

*D*ianna glanced at her watch as she entered the Mystic River Café and smiled when she spotted her friend at a nearby corner table.

"Abigayle Marks!"

Abbie stood to greet her friend with a hug. "Dianna! How nice to see you again. What's it been, three years?"

"Something like that," Dianna answered. "I bet the twins are really growing."

Abbie nodded. "They just turned twelve. Ian David is our wild child.... outgoing, loves to be outside, loves sports. Isabella, or Izzy, as we call her, is more reserved, quiet. She's more like me."

Abbie took a sip of her coffee. "When you called, you said you had a situation?"

Dianna nodded. "Yes, I have a 14-year-old girl. Her mom was killed three years ago in an accident caused by a drunk driver. She was in the car, and her leg was crushed. She had several surgeries, and as a result, wears a brace. Her father has never been in her life, and she has no other known family, so she was brought to Kiddy Korners Children's Home. In the three years I've known her, she has been somewhat withdrawn. She shuts down when anyone talks about her mother or the accident. She doesn't interact with the other children. Or at least not any more than she can help. She is among the oldest children there, and she believes only babies and the youngest children will be adopted. Our foster homes have no current openings, so I have no choice but to keep her at Kiddy Korners."

"Wow. Poor kid. I know how she feels." Abbie said softly.

Dianna nodded and said, "That's kind of why I called. You lived several years in a children's home as well. I thought maybe you would have ideas or suggestions as to how to help her. I want to find a way to get her to start enjoying life again, find something she enjoys doing. Her mom died shortly before Christmas, so she––"

"Hates Christmas," Abbie said, finishing her friend's sentence."

Dianna nodded again. "Yes. How did you move forward after you lost your parents? I mean, what helped you?"

Abbie was silent for a moment as she thought back to her own childhood. After losing her parents in a house fire at the age of ten, and with no family members able to take her in, she was sent to live in a children's home as well.

"I thought the world had ended," Abbie said softly as the memories came back to her. "I was angry at everyone...my parents for leaving me, God, for taking them. I was sure I would never enjoy life again...I wasn't sure I wanted to. I mean, my parents were gone, what more did I have left?" She paused for a moment, took a deep breath, then continued. "Everyone at the center tried to help, but I didn't want their help. They couldn't take away my pain, they couldn't mend my broken heart. It was like I had built a wall around myself. I was determined that no one would break down my wall."

"I can only imagine how awful that must have been for you," Dianna said sympathetically. "Sounds so much like Sofie. So, what helped you?"

Abbie paused for a moment as she thought back to the darkest days of her childhood. "A family of one of my friends at school sort of adopted me. And I spent time seeing a grief counselor. It was a way to sort out my feelings, to deal with the grief."

"IAN, do you remember my friend Dianna Wellington?" Abbie asked as she slipped into bed beside her husband later that night.

"Yeah, she's a social worker, right?"

Abbie nodded. "Yep. I had lunch with her today." Ian put down the book he was reading and turned his attention to his wife.

Abbie continued. "She was telling me about a case she has, a fourteen-year-old girl." She told him the story of young Sofie, and why her friend had asked for her help. "I was her at that age, and it got me to thinking."

"Thinking about what?" Ian questioned.

"Christmas. And the twins. Have you seen their Christmas lists?" Ian nodded. "Yes, looks like the toy department at Walmart." He chuckled. "I don't think Santa's sleigh can hold it all."

"I think it's time they learn the real meaning of Christmas, that it isn't all about gifts, that it's about helping others, doing good things for others. They need to learn that not everyone is as well off as they are, not everyone has the means to get what they want for Christmas."

"That's all fine and good," Ian replied, "Do you have something specific in mind?"

Abbie nodded her head. "I thought that maybe we can do something for Sofie, the one Dianna told me about, and the rest of the children at the center. She needs our help."

"Are you thinking about taking her in or something?"

"No. Maybe...I don't know." Abbie answered with a yawn. "I'll have to sleep on it and see what I can come up with. With only a few weeks until Christmas, we need to get our plan in motion. Teaching them to be kind to others is a gift we can give to them, one that they will have for the rest of their lives."

"Well, I think that's a great idea." Ian gave her a quick kiss on the cheek, then turned out the lamp on the nightstand beside the bed.

Ten minutes later, Ian had closed his eyes and was drifting off to sleep when Abbie suddenly sat up and shouted, "I've got it!"

"Whatever you've got, don't give it to me." Ian chuckled at his own joke.

Abbie swatted him on the arm. "No, I think I have an idea. We could give the kids at the center an old-fashioned

Christmas—you know, hayrides, Christmas Carols around the bonfire, the whole nine yards."

Ian was silent for a moment as he pondered the idea.

"That's a good idea. Now how about we get some sleep?" Ian yawned.

"I'll call Dianna tomorrow. I'll bet she will have some good suggestions for the kids." Abbie said.

"I'm sure she will. Now let's let it rest till morning." Ian said as drifted off to sleep.

Abbie smiled to herself as she snuggled under the warm blankets and closed her eyes in sleep.

3 - SOFIE'S CHRISTMAS MIRACLE

*A*fter a couple of days of thinking about what they could do for Sofie and the other children at the center, Abbie approached Dianna with the idea of giving the children an old-fashioned Christmas. Dianna thought it was a splendid idea.

The next couple of weeks were a flurry of activity for the Marks family as they worked to get their farm ready for the children.

Finally, the day before the big event had arrived.

"So, Mom, tell me again why we are doing this." Isabella continued brushing her horse while Abbie hung up red and green crepe paper on the walls and in the horse stalls.

"Your dad and I felt that it would be good for you and your brother to experience what it is like to help others and to learn that not all children are as fortunate. These children don't have parents who love them or a house with their own room. We wanted to reach out to these children, show them they are special, that someone cares. We'll give them a day they will remember for the rest of their lives."

Isabella was quiet for a moment as she thought about her mother's words.

"Mom?"

"Yes?"

"Did someone do that for you after Grandpa and Grandma died in that fire?" Isabella asked softly.

"When I was sent to the children's home, I had to switch schools. My first friend was a girl named Hayley. She invited me to spend a night at her house. Her parents just sort of unofficially adopted me. They showed me that it was okay for me to love again and open my heart to be loved again. They could never take the place of my parents, but they cared about me like my parents did."

"Whatever happened to them?" Isabella questioned. "Why haven't I met them?"

"Well, actually, honey, you did when you were little," Abbie answered. Isabella shook her head. "I don't remember them."

"No, I don't suppose you would. Hayley got married several years ago and moved to Germany with her husband who Is in the Army. We write to each other a few times a year and exchange pictures."

Isabella was thoughtful for a moment. "Do you think maybe I can be friends with some of the kids that come tomorrow?" Abbie smiled.

"That's very possible, Sweetheart. Let's show these kids the best time ever." Arm in arm, Mother and daughter left the barn and headed towards the house.

DIANNA ARRIVED at Kiddy Korners promptly at nine a.m. Saturday morning, the day of the big event. She smiled as she entered the Commons area. The room was loud, with the excited chatter of the children.

"Oh, Dianna, I'm so glad you're here," Kathryn said as she came down the stairs and into the Commons. "Someone refuses to go. I can't get her to budge."

Dianna sighed. "And by someone you mean, Sofie?"

Kat nodded. "I've tried everything I could think of. I guess I could stay back with her."

Dianna shook her head. "No one is staying back with her. She is going," Dianna said, with determination. "We will be right down."

Kat was doubtful but only shook her head in exasperation. Sofie was a strong-willed little girl, and often stubborn. Once she made up her mind, it often couldn't be changed.

DIANNA DIDN'T BOTHER to knock on the door. She opened it and entered the bedroom. Sofie was lying on her bed, staring up at the ceiling.

Dianna sat down on the edge of the bed. "Wanna talk about it?"

"Talk about what?" Sofie asked softly, knowing perfectly well what her case manager was implying.

"I'm pretty sure you know what I mean. There is a room full of kids downstairs waiting to load the bus to go to the farm. And here you are, alone in your room, making everyone else wait for you."

"They don't have to wait. I'm not going," Sofie answered.

"And why not?" Dianna asked. "It will be fun. My friend and her family went to a lot of work to give you children a fun day away from your daily routine and activities. I'm sure you will have a good time once you get there. You need to give it a chance, Sofie."

Sofie was silent for a moment, then sat up. "Well, I guess I could go along and help watch the younger kids. But that's it. Don't expect me to have fun. A farm has nothing but a bunch of stinky animals. I'm sure the kids will love it."

Dianna tried to hide her smile. "Fair enough. Now let's get downstairs and load the bus."

Sofie followed Dianna from the room, still unsure about this farm day.

4 - SOFIE'S CHRISTMAS MIRACLE

"*M*om, when are they going to be here?" Isabella asked, staring out the window.

Abbie sighed. "They will be here soon. They won't get here any faster by you asking me every five minutes when they are going to be here. Where's your brother?"

Isabella shrugged. "Beats me. The last time I saw him, he was—HERE THEY COME!" Isabella shouted. She turned from the window and bolted out the door, letting the door slam shut behind her.

Abbie shook her head and couldn't help but smile at her young daughter's excitement. "Ian David! They're here! Let's go!" Abbie said.

Ian David came into the kitchen. "Awww Mom, do I have to go out there?" He took a bite of his apple. "It's Saturday; I always hang out with the guys. Can't Izzy just play with these kids?"

"Ian David, we have been through this. You can give up one Saturday out of the year to help give these kids a

Christmas to remember. These kids don't have families or a home of their own. Your Christmas list is a mile long. These kids are lucky if they get even one gift." Abbie put her arm around her young son as they walked outside together. "We have the means of doing something nice for these kids, and your father and I feel that it would be a good experience for you and your sister to learn what it is like to give instead of always receiving. I know you would rather be with your friends, but I'm asking you to do your best to help these kids have a good day….and without an attitude."

Ian David sighed, knowing perfectly well there was no point in arguing. It would be a losing battle. "Okay, I'll do what I can to help them have a good day."

Abbie smiled as they arrived at the end of the driveway just as the bus came to a stop.

DIANNA WAS the first to get off the bus. She smiled and greeted her friend with a hug. "Hello, Abbie. I can't tell you how excited these kids are."

"Hi, Dianna. You remember my husband, Ian, and the twins, Ian David, and Isabella?"

Dianna nodded as she shook hands with Ian, then the twins. "So nice to see you again. I can't tell you how thrilled we are to be here. Thank you so much for what you are doing for these kids."

Ian smiled. "We are glad to do it. We have hayrides, a little petting zoo area, and later as it begins to get dark, a bonfire for roasting marshmallows."

"Can the kids get out of the bus now?" Isabella asked.

Dianna smiled. "Ok, kids, come on out!" Within seconds, loud excited laughter filled the air as twenty-five children bounded down the bus steps along with six adults. "Let me introduce you to the staff that will be helping out today." She introduced them while the kids waited eagerly.

Abbie smiled warmly as she nodded hello. "Nice to meet all of you. Thank you so much for coming today."

"Ok, kids, listen up!" Ian said loudly to be heard above the excited chatter. "The goal for today is to be safe and have fun. We will start by giving you a tour of the farm, so you will know where things are. If you need to use the bathroom, there is one in the barn. Now, let's start in the barn, and we will introduce you to the horses."

"Can we ride them?" Eight-year-old Shayla asked in a loud voice.

Ian nodded. "Yes, anyone that wants to ride will get a chance to do so."

"Cool!" She said, her brown eyes dancing with excitement.

As the children followed Ian to the barn, Isabella noticed a girl who looked older than the other children, walking slowly behind the others. Her head was lowered, and her steps were hesitant as she was wearing a leg brace. Isabella pulled back from the others and approached the girl.

"Hi. I'm Isabella. What's your name?" The girl looked up but remained silent. Isabella noticed the sadness in her blue eyes. "Welcome to our farm. We have lots of animals, and tonight we're gonna have a bonfire and roast marshmallows and sing Christmas songs, and––"

"I didn't want to come," the girl replied angrily. "They made me. I don't like stinky animals. I don't like Christmas. And I don't like you. Now just leave me alone."

Isabella stared in disbelief as the girl turned and ran surprisingly fast, even with her leg brace, towards the house.

Why did I have to come? Sofie thought. As far as she was concerned, her world had ended the day her mother had died. Tears blurred her vision. She arrived at the house and sat down on the porch swing. In the distance, she could see Isabella still watching her. For a moment, she felt bad for the way she had spoken to her but shook it off—she didn't care. She didn't want to be here. She looked around at her surroundings and noticed a grove of trees behind the house. She glanced towards the barn, noticing that Isabella was no longer watching her. She got up and hurried into the trees. She hadn't gone very far when she noticed a treehouse built among the trees.

She smiled to herself. *They'll never find me here.* Sofie climbed the ladder and slipped inside her newfound hideout.

Isabella saw her sit on the swing and turned around to catch up with her dad and the other children. As she arrived at the barn, she ran into Dianna Wellington.

"Hi, Isabella. Have you seen Sofie?"

"I don't know who Sofie is, but a girl with a leg brace ran towards the house. Says she doesn't like Christmas. Or stinky animals. Or me. She--"

Dianna sighed. "That's Sofie. Where did you say she went?"

Isabella pointed, then noticed that Sofie was no longer sitting in the swing. "She was there a minute ago. She looked really sad."

"We'd better find her. Will you help look for her?"

Isabella nodded. "Ian David will help too. I'll get him."

As Isabella ran towards the barn to get her brother, Dianna looked nervously around the farm. *Where could Sofie have gone?* It was a large farm, and there were many places to hide. Sofie was a clever girl and could easily hide where she wouldn't be found. Dianna felt sick at the thought of Sofie somewhere out there alone.

"Oh, Sofie. Where are you?" She whispered softly.

At that moment, Ian and his children came running from the barn. "Abbie will stay with the kids. We'll go look for Sofie. Dianna, you stay by the house in case she comes back."

Dianna nodded as Ian, Isabella, and Ian David separated and went in three different directions.

ISABELLA HAD BEEN WALKING through the woods for about ten minutes when she stopped and looked around. No sign of Sofie anywhere. She continued walking, then stopped again, this time listening carefully, when she heard soft cries coming from a short distance away. *The treehouse,* she thought. *Why didn't I think of that?* She hurried over and climbed up the ladder. She spotted Sofie huddled in a corner, arms wrapped around her knees, crying.

"Sofie?"

"What are you doing here? The idea was for me to get away from you. And everyone else. Can't you people just leave me alone?"

"My dad and brother are looking for you too. Mrs. Wellington is worried about you." Isabella sat down on the floor beside her. "Why are you crying?" Isabella gently asked.

"Who says I'm crying?" Sofie retorted.

"I know crying when I see it," Isabella answered. "What's wrong?"

Sofie was silent for a few moments. Isabella seemed like a nice girl. But could she trust her? She had no one in her life that she felt that she could confide in.

"What's wrong?" Isabella asked again.

"Three years ago, right before Christmas, my mom was killed in a car accident by a drunk driver. Ever since then, I've hated Christmas. It was Mom's favorite holiday. But after the accident..." Sofie's voice drifted off.

"What about your dad?"

Sofie shrugged. "I don't have one. Mom told me he died, and she didn't want to talk about it."

"Wow. I can't imagine not having my dad here." Isabella said softly. "What was your mom's name? I bet she was pretty." Sofie nodded.

"She was. Her name was Kaylie. Kaylie Rose. She was my best friend."

"So, you've been at this children's place ever since?"

Sofie nodded. "Yeah. I'm fourteen, and most of the kids are younger. Most people don't want to adopt kids my age."

Isabella was silent for a moment as she thought about

what she had said. Sofie seemed like a nice girl, and she felt sorry for her. She didn't know what she would do if she didn't have her parents or her twin brother. She shuddered at the thought. "Sofie, you should come back to the farm. We're missing all the fun." Isabella smiled. "I'll introduce you to my horse."

Sofie took a deep breath. Isabella was a nice girl, and she couldn't help but like her.

"Please, Sofie. You'll have fun. Your mom would want you to."

Isabella was right. Her mom would want her to enjoy this day. She hadn't thought of that. "Okay, I'll go," Sofie said softly.

"I can't wait for the bonfire," Isabella said with excitement as she and her new friend left the treehouse together.

"This was a wonderful idea," Dianna told her friend Abbie later that afternoon. "And such a special treat for these kids. We've always given them a Christmas party, but this is by far the best Christmas ever for them."

Abbie smiled. "It was good for my kids too. At first, Ian David wanted no part in this. He wanted to spend the day with his friends like he does every Saturday. But look at him. He's having a blast." Abbie pointed to where her son was tossing a football around with several other boys.

Dianne glanced around until she spotted Sofie sitting on the ground, chatting with Isabella. "Looks like Sofie made a friend in your daughter. She usually sits off by herself."

Abbie glanced over to where Dianna was looking. "Izzy has a couple of friends at school, but they don't live close by, so she spends a lot of time riding her horse or curling up with a book."

"Most of the kids at the center have their own little groups, but Sofie seldom spends time with the other kids. She spends a lot of time alone in her room. She is reserved. In the three years that I have been her case manager, this is the most I have seen her interact with anyone she didn't know.

Abbie nodded in understanding. She had been that way too after the death of her parents. She had been afraid to get close to anyone for fear that they too would leave her.

"And she has no other family?" Abbie asked after a moment.

Dianna shook her head. "None that we know of. Her mother was an only child, with no other family we know of, and there is no information about her father. She says her mom never talked about her him at all."

"What will become of her if she doesn't get adopted?"

"Once she turns 18, she can no longer remain at the center. When she enters high school, many of her classes will be focused on teaching her life skills to help her make it on her own in the adult world.

Abbie shook her head. "That's so sad. I mean, she seems like such a nice girl. All she needs is someone to love her, take care of her, and show her that it is ok to love again without letting the memory of her mother die. "

"I agree," Dianna answered. "But the older children tend to be overlooked. Many people go for the younger ones.

They miss out on a lot of wonderful children who just want to be loved and have a family of their own. Like Sofie."

"What about a foster home? Couldn't she be placed? At least then, she would be with a family."

Dianna sighed. "Right after the accident, she was placed in an emergency placement foster home until a bed became available at the center. An emergency placement home is only licensed for ninety days. We often get kids with no warning at all, such as with Sofie. She needs a family and a home to call her own. They all do."

Abbie nodded. "Looks like Ian is getting the bonfire ready." She said. "The kids have been looking forward to this."

Dianna smiled. "They sure have."

"Let's go 'round up the troops," Abbie said with a laugh.

The two longtime friends headed across the yard to gather the children for the long-awaited bonfire that would end their fun day at the Marks farm.

The children gathered in a circle around the bonfire. Izzy sat beside her new friend, Sofie. Ian took his place in the circle and picked up his guitar.

Sofie listened to the music around her, but her thoughts wandered. She had had a good time here at the farm, and she was happy that she now had a new friend.

But she knew that soon this wonderful day would end, and she would go back to her mundane life at the center. She was glad it was dark, so no-one could see her eyes were wet.

"Sofie, maybe I can come to visit you at the center one day," Izzy said. "I'm sure Mom and Dad would say it was okay."

"I would like that," Sofie said softly. She wondered if Izzy really would visit her. People often promised they would visit, but then never did. She hoped that Izzy meant what she said, but was afraid to get her hopes up, for fear of being let down.

All too soon, it was time to board the bus and head back to the Center. Izzy walked beside her friend, both silent until they reached the door of the bus.

"I-I had a nice time," Sofie said, barely above a whisper. "I hope we can keep in touch." Izzy nodded.

"For sure. I can come visit you, and maybe you can come here to spend a weekend or something." Sofie stepped into the bus, stopped, then turned back to Izzy, embracing her in a hug. "Bye, Izzy." She turned and got into the bus.

A short distance away, Dianna was standing with Abbie and had witnessed this rare emotion from Sofie.

"Wow! I have never seen her like this. It's amazing."

"She and Izzy really hit it off," Abbie answered. Dianna said goodbye to her friend, then got onto the bus. She took her seat beside Sofie. As the bus pulled away from the farm, Sofie turned towards Dianna. "Thank you…for bringing me here, Dianna. I had a nice time."

Dianna smiled. "I'm glad you did, Sweetheart."

5 - SOFIE'S CHRISTMAS MIRACLE

*I*an poured himself a cup of coffee and sat down across the table from his wife. The morning chores were done, and they knew very shortly that their quiet time alone together would come to an end.

"Well, I would say yesterday was a huge success," Abbie said.

Ian nodded in agreement. "Even Ian David seemed to enjoy the day. Not bad for someone who was dead set against participating."

"And Izzy seemed to really enjoy that girl, Sofie. Dianna said that Sofie is usually withdrawn and seldom interacts with the other children, so she was thrilled to see her hanging out with Izzy."

Before Ian could say another word, they heard the thundering footsteps of the twins having their usual morning race down the stairs.

"I won!" Izzy shouted as she took her place at the table.

Ian David stuck his tongue out as he took his place beside

his sister.

"Perfect timing. Breakfast is ready," Abbie said as she got up to dish up their plates.

Ian took a sip of his coffee.

"So, what did you two get out of the day yesterday? Ian David, you go first." Ian said as he put his cup down.

Ian David was thoughtful for a moment as he thought about the boys he had spent time with the day before. "I met some real neat guys. They like sports and video games." Ian David paused, then continued. "I kinda feel sorry for them, though. I mean, they live with all these other kids. They share a room with four others and never really have their own space. They have no time to hang out with friends. They can't go anywhere without the staff with them."

Ian nodded in agreement as his son continued. "And they don't have parents to tuck them in at night. It's really sad, Dad. I hope I can play with them again. They were really fun."

"We'll see what we can do," Ian answered, then turned his attention to his young daughter. "How about you, Izzy? What did you get out of the day?"

"It was great, Dad," Isabella said without hesitation. "I met this cool girl named Sofie. She's fourteen, only two years older than me. Her mom was killed in a car accident. She's never had a dad." Abbie opened her mouth to speak, but Isabella continued, barely taking a breath. "Her mom was her best friend. And she had the coolest name…Kaylie Rose. Isn't that the most beautiful name? She said--"

"W-what did you say her name was?" Ian interrupted, the color suddenly draining from his face.

'Kaylie Rose,' Isabella said.

Abbie immediately noticed the change in her husband's demeanor, "Ian, what in the world is wrong with you? You look liked you've seen a ghost."

"Uh…nothing. I'm fine. I…uh…I forgot something in the barn. Excuse me." Abbie and the twins stared at him as he hurried out the door.

Ian David looked at his mother. "What's with Dad?"

"I have no idea," Abbie answered. "I'll go find out. You kids stay here and finish your breakfast. I'll be back in a few minutes." With that, she followed him out the door. Isabella looked at her brother and shrugged.

"Parents. Sometimes I just don't understand them."

Ian David nodded in agreement.

ABBIE GLANCED around the barn and spotted her husband at the end of the long row of stalls, staring out the window. She watched him in silence for a moment, then approached him. "Hey Cowboy," she said, a definite note of concern in her voice. "What happened in there?" When Ian didn't answer, Abbie continued. "Honey, what's wrong? You look like you've seen a ghost. Even the kids could tell something was wrong. Please, Ian. What is it?"

After another moment of silence, Ian finally turned to face her. Abbie was taken aback by the look on her husband's face, a look she had never seen before. Ian reached out and took her hands in his. "Abbie, what I have to say isn't easy. I-I don't know where to start––"

"IAN, you're scaring me. Please just tell me."

Ian took a deep breath then slowly let it out. "I know I maybe should have told you this before, but it happened before we met. I had just bought this farm when I met this girl. We seemed to hit it off and started dating. I thought she was the one for me. We had been dating a couple of months, and I thought it was getting serious. We…" Ian took a breath, then continued. "Then one day she just left. I didn't know where she had gone or anything. A few days later, I got a letter from her saying that she wasn't cut out to be a farmer's wife, and she was sorry. She said she was happier as a city girl." Ian paused briefly, then continued, "Maybe I should have picked up on her dislike for the farm life, but I didn't." Ian took a deep breath and slowly let it out before continuing. "I tried calling her, but her phone had been disconnected. She didn't have any family that I knew of."

"But Ian, I don't understand why you are bringing this up. I mean, we've been together all these years. What happened then has nothing to do with now. Everyone has a past. And that's where it needs to stay…in the past."

"Her name was Kaylie Rose," Ian said slowly.

Abbie stared at him for a moment, the shock on her face evident. "What? Kaylie Rose––like Sofie's mother?"

Ian nodded. "Kaylie Rose McKenna."

Abbie sat down on a nearby hay bale. She opened her mouth to speak, but the words were stuck around the lump in her throat as she read between the lines of what her husband was saying. "Are…are you saying that Sofie is your daughter?" She finally asked, her voice barely above a whisper.

"I'm saying it is a possibility," Ian said quietly.

The silence that followed was deafening.

"Why wouldn't she have told you if you were the father of her baby?" Abbie asked, a little more forcefully than she intended. Having a prior girlfriend was one thing, but a child…?

Ian shook his head. "I-I don't know." He said softly. "We never talked about kids. But one night, just before she left, we got carried away and well… I guess maybe she got scared. I don't know."

"So, you think Sofie–"

"The timing is an awful coincidence. If she did get pregnant, well, the child would be about Sofie's age. Maybe she thought I would be angry. Or maybe she disliked farm life enough—"

Abby turned and went back to the house without saying another word.

IAN TOOK A DEEP BREATH, then opened the door to the bedroom. It had been a couple of hours since he had shared his suspicions with his wife about the possibility that he could be Sofie's father. He found Abbie sitting on the window seat. "Um…. honey, can we talk?"

"Ian, I'm sorry I ran out the way I did. It's just that—"

"You don't need to explain. I understand. It was a bomb I dropped on you. When Izzy talked about Sofie and told us her mother's name—well, Kaylie Rose is not a common name. It was so long ago. A part of my life I had pretty much forgotten about."

"She was part of your past. I get that," Abbie stated firmly. But if you think you are her father, we need to find out for sure."

"When Kaylie left…I didn't even consider she could be pregnant. I…" Ian's voice trailed off.

"I believe you…that you didn't know," Abbie said softly. "Because if you had, you would have done whatever you could to take care of both Kaylie and the baby. You wouldn't just let her go. I know you."

"W-what if we find out I am her father?" Ian asked.

Abbie took her husband's hands in hers. "She needs a family. She has lived in the children's center because she had no known relatives. But if we find out that you are her father, she needs to be with us."

Ian put his arms around his wife. "Thank you for being supportive. I know it can't be easy knowing that I may have another child—"

"It happened years ago, Ian. Like I said, we all have a past. There's nothing to be sorry about."

"You are amazing, Abbie. What do we do now?"

"Shortly before you came in, I called Dianna to find out what's next. She and Sofie will meet us tomorrow to take a DNA test. Then we will know for sure."

Ian sighed heavily, feeling as though a huge weight had been lifted from his shoulders.

6 - SOFIE'S CHRISTMAS MIRACLE

*A*bbie slowly opened her eyes, now awake with a strange feeling. She reached over for her husband, but her arm hit his empty pillow. She squinted in the darkness to glance at the clock on the nightstand beside the bed. *3:40 a.m.*

"Ian?" When she received no answer, she put her robe on and wandered out into the dark hallway. She saw the light underneath the door to the computer room. She paused outside the door for a moment before opening it and stepping quietly inside. "Ian? What are you doing up at this hour?"

Ian turned his chair to face her." "I was just thinking. Sorry if I woke you."

Abbie shook her head. "You didn't. I woke up, and you weren't there. What are you doing?"

"I was just thinking. They said we should get the test results back later this week."

Abbie sat down in the chair across from him. "How do you feel about this?"

"I don't know. I'm going to find out whether or not I have another child. Sofie is fourteen years old. She is a teenager... I don't know anything about raising a teenager. How do I parent a child her age when we are basically strangers? We know nothing about each other."

Abbie reached over and took his hands in her own. "Honey, if Sofie is your child, we will raise her together. We will learn together. We will make mistakes, just like all parents do. But we won't treat her like a stranger. We won't treat her any differently than we do the twins."

"And what about the twins? This will disrupt their lives also. They are used to it just being them. I don't know how they will deal with having another kid around. I don't know how Izzy will like having to share her room, at least until we can figure out a way to give Sofie her own room." Ian paused to take a breath, and Abbie jumped in.

"She will adjust. She might even like having to share her room. They got along well when all the kids were here. Let's not create problems until the problem arises. Christmas is next week. Just think how wonderful it would be for Sofie if we find out you are her biological father, and we can bring her home for Christmas. What a wonderful Christmas gift that would be for her. And for us."

Ian smiled. He couldn't help but admire his wife's support and enthusiasm. "Thank you, Abbie, for being so supportive. I know this won't be easy for you. I mean--"

"I know what you mean," Abbie said softly, interrupting. "But Sweetheart, you are my husband, and I love you. And if the test shows that you are her father, then her place is here with us. Even if I am not her biological mother, that doesn't mean I won't love her." Abbie paused, then continued. "She spent three years with no parents or family. If she is your child, we need to bring her home."

Tears glistened in his eyes as he put his arms around her. He tried to speak but couldn't. His wife understood what he was trying to say.

LATER THAT AFTERNOON, Abbie was sitting at the kitchen table, a cup of coffee in her hand. Her mind was a flurry of thoughts about the possibility of bringing another child into their home. Part of her was excited at the thought of having another daughter, but another part of her was wasn't quite so sure. It would definitely mean some major changes in their lives. She took a sip of her coffee.

Her thoughts were interrupted by the slamming of the front door, and seconds later, Isabella ran into the kitchen. "Mom, do you think Sofie really is my sister?"

Abbie slowly shrugged her shoulders. "I don't know, Honey. It's a possibility. How would you feel if it turns out she is your sister? It would mean making a lot of changes."

Izzy was quiet for a moment as she thought about her Mom's question. "Well, I really had fun with her when she was here. I felt sorry for her too. I mean, she lives with all those kids, she has no family or anything. I can't even imagine living without you, Dad and Ian David. Or living any place besides this farm. Or having my own horse."

"It would mean sharing your room. At least till we could figure out something else."

Izzy shrugged. "That's okay. I've always wanted a sister."

"Well, I didn't." Izzy and Abbie glanced towards the door as Ian David entered the room, slamming the door behind him. "One sister is enough," he added. "Does she have to come and live with us?"

"Yes, we've talked about this, Ian David. If we find out that she is your father's daughter, she will come to live with us. How would you like to live in a place with no parents or family, and then find out you have a father, but you still have to live in the children's center?"

"How about you, Mom? How do you feel about it?" Izzy asked as she sat down at the table.

Abbie smiled. "I think this will be a big change for all of us. But we need to be supportive of your dad. It will be a huge adjustment. We will all need to work as a team to make Sofie welcome and make her feel like she is part of the family. We'll need to give her time to adjust to us too."

UNKNOWN TO ANY OF THEM, Ian was standing in the kitchen doorway, a piece of paper in his hand. "The results are in," he said, barely above a whisper. His family turned to face him, waiting for him to continue. Silently he took his place at the table. He glanced at Abbie, then at his children.

"Read it, Dad," Isabella said eagerly. "Is Sofie our sister?"

Ian took a deep breath, then read the words that would change their lives forever:

Dear Mr. Marks:

In the case of fourteen-year-old Sofie Melissa McKenna, the probability of you being her biological father is 99.99%.

Silence followed as each member of the family let the news sink in. "I'll call Dianna," Abbie said, finally breaking the silence. She excused herself as she left the room to make the call. She returned a few minutes later. "I told Dianna we would go today to talk to Sofie. She will meet us there."

"Will she be coming home with us today?" Izzy asked.

"I don't know, honey," Abbie answered. "We'll need to see what Dianna says, and, more importantly, how Sofie feels. This is going to be a shock to her. She may feel that she needs time to think the situation over before she makes a decision."

Ian David scowled. "I had a lot of things on my Christmas list, but I don't remember a sister being one of them."

"Well, I think having an older sister will be awesome," his twin retorted.

Ian looked sternly at his son. "I expect you to behave and welcome her into our home. After all, this will be her home, too, from now on."

"Yes, Sir." Ian David answered, then excused himself and stomped up the stairs to his room. Izzy couldn't hide her excitement. "Can we go get her now? Do we get to tell her that she is my sister? Do you think she will like it here? I can teach her to ride my horse."

Abbie laughed. "Slow down, young lady. We will go shortly. I'm sure she will like having you for a sister." Izzy jumped up from the table. "I'm going to tell Schatze all about my sister," she said, referring to her horse. Without another word, she ran outside.

Abbie looked at her husband, who was still staring down at the paper he held in his hand. She walked around the table and put her arms around him.

"Let's get ready to bring our daughter home."

"Thank you, sweetheart, for accepting my daughter."

Abbie smiled. "From this moment on, she is *our* daughter." With that, Ian and Abbie walked hand in hand upstairs to begin preparations to welcome their new daughter into their family.

7 - SOFIE'S CHRISTMAS MIRACLE

The family parked in front of the Kiddy Korners Children's Center. Isabella was the first out of the car. "Come on, guys. Let's go."

She headed towards the door, but her mother's stern voice made her stop.

"Isabella Dawn, you stop right there. We are not going to run in like a herd of elephants. I know you are anxious, but I think your dad needs to go talk to her first."

Isabella waited patiently for the rest of her family to catch up to her, then opened the door to the center. Dianna was waiting and greeted them with a smile. "Good afternoon, everyone."

"Dianna, is it possible to take Sofie home today? Abbie questioned. "I know there will be legal stuff and paperwork we need to do."

"I spoke to my supervisor and explained the situation, and he gave the authorization to allow Sofie to spend the holidays with your family. Then after New Year's, we will have you begin the paperwork to release her to your permanent custody. There will need to be a home study. Just a formality required by the state. We contacted the state-licensing department and explained the situation, and they agreed that under the unique circumstances, we can give you an emergency foster care license." Ian and Abbie nodded in understanding. "I thought maybe you and Ian could go talk to Sofie first," Abbie said. "The twins and I will wait here. We don't want her to be overwhelmed by all of us barging into her room."

"That sounds good," Dianna replied, then turned to Ian. "Let's go talk to your daughter." Ian nodded, then followed Dianna up the stairs.

Dianna knocked on a door at the end of the hallway. When she received no answer, she opened the door and went in. Ian followed.

"Hi, Sofie," Dianna said.

Sofie was lying on her bed, hands behind her head. "Hi, What're you doing here?" Sofie asked, her eyes on Ian.

Ian cleared his throat, nervously. "Hi, Sofie. I was wondering if I could talk to you." Sofie was thoughtful for a moment, then sat up.

"Yeah, I guess." Dianna and Ian sat down on either side of her. Ian cleared his throat again. "Sofie, do you remember that test we took where they swabbed the inside of our mouths?"

"Yeah, so?" Sofie folded her arms across her chest.

Ian continued. "The reason we did that was to find out if you and I might be related. We got the results back." Ian paused for a moment. *"Sofie, I am your father,"* Ian said softly.

Sofie stared at him for a moment, then shook her head. "No! You can't be my father. I don't have a father. If I did, my mother would have told me. You're lying."

Ian glanced at Dianna, his eyes pleading for help.

Dianna put her arms around the girl. "Sofie, Mr. Marks is telling the truth. He is your biological father."

Sofie was quiet for a moment as she pondered this news. When she looked up, tears were streaming down her cheeks. "Why did you leave us? When I was little, I asked Mom where my father was. She said you were dead. So why are you here now? And what made you even think that you are my father anyway?"

In the easiest way possible that she would understand, Ian explained how he had come to suspect that he was her father, after hearing her mother's name. When he had finished, Sofie looked at him but was silent for several moments as she thought about what she had just heard.

Dianna placed a hand on her shoulder. "Sofie? What do you think?" She asked gently.

"My mom lied to me," Sofie said softly.

Ian shook his head. "No, honey. She was only wanting to protect you from getting hurt. If she told you your father was dead, then you wouldn't go through life wondering where he was."

"Why did you leave us?" Sofie asked again.

"Honey, I didn't leave you. I didn't know about you. I had just bought the farm when I met your mom. We had only been dating for about a couple of months. But I guess she didn't want to live on a farm, because one day she just left. She didn't tell me where she was going or that she was expecting a baby. I don't know why she didn't tell me about you. Maybe she thought it would be better or easier that way. If I had known, I would have made sure that you were taken care of."

Sofie was quiet as she looked from Ian to Dianna. "So...so what happens now?"

Ian sat down on the bed beside her and took her hands in his own. "Sofie, my family and I would like you to come and live with us. We want you to be part of our family. That is, if you will have us."

"Mom, is Sofie gonna come live with us?" Ian David questioned as he sat down in the nearest chair.

Abbie sat down on the couch across from him. "I'm hoping she does. Does that bother you?" Ian David shrugged, not knowing what to say. Abbie waited for him to answer.

"Well, I still think one sister is enough. Where will she sleep?"

Before Abbie could answer, his twin sister jumped into the conversation. "She'll sleep in my room, you said. Right, mom?"

"Yes, until we can work something else out."

"Great!" Isabella said excitedly. "My friend Aimee shares a room with her older sister, and she says it's great because they lay awake talking late into the night and share secrets. I think having an older sister will be cool."

Abbie smiled at her daughter's enthusiasm. "I'm glad to hear that, sweetheart." She turned her attention back to her son. "I know this won't be easy. It will be an adjustment for all of us. But just think about how Sofie must feel. She spent her life thinking her father was dead, and now she finds out she has a dad. She spent three years living here with no family at all. It will take time for all of us to get to know each other. But we can't just leave her here. How would you feel if you were in her place?'

Ian David was thoughtful for a moment. "I guess I would feel like no one cared."

Abbie nodded. "I'm sure that is how Sofie feels."

"Why does she wear a brace on her leg?" Isabella asked. "I asked Sofie, but she changed the subject and wouldn't answer. "

"Dianna told me that her leg was crushed in the accident that killed her mother. She had several surgeries and some physical therapy, but she gave up on the therapy and wouldn't work at getting better. She refused to continue. The therapist felt that if she had continued her therapy, her leg would have gotten stronger and healed more quickly, then she might have been able to get rid of the brace."

Isabella was thoughtful for a moment, and said, "Mom, do you think she will go back to physical therapy? If I go with her?"

"Well, we can sure talk to her about it. But I think it best we wait until she gets settled in." Abbie turned her attention back to her son. "How about it, Ian David? Are you willing to give it a try?"

He sighed heavily. "Yeah, I guess so," then added, "I guess it might not be so bad having an older sister."

Abbie put an arm around each twin. "We can make this work if we all work together."

SOFIE WAS quiet for a moment as she thought about what her father had said. She looked up at him, her cheeks still wet with tears. "Y-you really want me to come live with you?"

Dianna quietly opened the door and slipped out into the hallway, returning seconds later, followed by Abbie, Izzy, and Ian David.

"Did you say yes? Are you going to come live with us and be my big sister?" Izzy asked excitedly

"I-I think I would like that," Sofie answered softly.

Abbie smiled as she knelt down and embraced her in a hug. "Welcome to our family, Sofie."

"Abbie, how about you and the twins help Sofie pack while Ian signs the release paperwork?"

"That sounds like a wonderful idea, Dianna."

Sofie waited until Dianna and Ian left the room, then said softly, "I-I can't call you Mom."

Abbie smiled warmly. "How about you just call me Abbie? Honey, I can't replace your mom. No one can do that. But I can be your friend. You never have to be afraid to talk to me about your mom."

"Really?"

Abbie nodded. "Of course, it's okay."

Sofie slowly reached out and put her arms around her. "Thank you, Abbie."

Abbie patted her on the back as she felt her own tears

coming on, then stood up and took her new daughter by the hand. "Let's get you packed, shall we?"

Sofie got her suitcase out of the closet and plopped it on the bed. She began removing her clothes from the closet. Abbie and Izzy started removing the clothes from the dresser. Even her new brother was helping.

She looked upward and thought, I love you, Mom. I will always carry you with me in my heart.

A short time later, Sofie said her goodbyes to Dianna and the other staff and children. She promised she would visit them and write soon. She joined her new family in the car and watched out the window until The Kiddy Korners Children's Center was no longer in sight.

For the first time since the accident that had taken her Mother's life, she felt that she would be okay. Her mother would always be a part of her, but now she had a dad and a family who loved her.

THE END

STORY FOUR

Lexi

1 - LEXI

*L*eif Konroy sat down on the corner of his desk and took a deep breath. "I'm sure you're wondering why I called you in for this meeting in person," he said to the couple sitting before him.

Toby Shores nodded, and asked the counselor of his daughter's elementary school, "Has one of the girls done something?" School had barely been in session for a month.

Leif shook his head. "No, they're not in trouble. But I'm concerned about Rylie. Her teacher has reported some difficulty with her. She seems to be withdrawn lately. For example, she'll sit alone at lunch, and sometimes on the playground. She has missed several homework assignments and her grades are starting to show it. Compared to last year, Rylie seems like a different girl, according to her teacher."

"Well, she has spent a lot of time in her room lately, but when I asked her about it, she said the homework is harder this year, and it takes more time." Beth paused a moment before continuing, "She and her sister Parker show some sibling rivalry, but that's normal, isn't it?" Beth replied, as she looked at her husband.

He nodded in agreement.

Leif walked around his desk and opened a folder that was lying on his desk. "I talked to her about it, but she insists there's nothing wrong. So, I've taken the liberty of speaking to Dr. Kaleb, our school psychologist. She believes that Rylie may be exhibiting signs of depression."

"Depression? What would she be depressed about?" Toby asked.

"Well, it's common for people, particularity children, to get depressed about things that go on in their lives, like a tragedy or a death in the family. May I ask, has anything like that affected your family?

"No, not at all," Beth said.

"That indicates Rylie's kind of depression may be different. It could be medical. If it is, then the symptoms would be beyond her control. I suggest you have her evaluated to see if she does suffer from depression. If so, there are medications that will help her. Counselors also."

Beth took a breath, trying to take in what the counselor was telling them.

"I recommend that you set up an appointment with Dr. Kaleb." Mr. Konroy continued, "She has several openings in the next few days.

"Thank you so much for your help, Mr. Konroy. We will do that." Beth said.

Her husband nodded in agreement as he stood to leave.

Mr. Konroy stood and shook Toby's hand, then Beth's.

"Don't hesitate to call if you need any more assistance. We all want what is best for Rylie."

"Thank you again," Beth said as she and her husband left the office. They walked the rest of the way to the car in silence.

⁓◦꧁꧂◦⁓

"So, what did Dr. Kaleb say?" Toby asked when Beth got home after Rylie's appointment the next day.

Beth sighed. "She said it's possible she is depressed, although Rylie didn't open up to her as much as he'd like. You know how stubborn she can be."

"That she can be."

Beth gave Toby the rundown on the rest of the visit. Dr. Kaleb had suggested they take her to a specialist for therapy, before considering the medication option. Beth learned that some of the side effects for a child Rylie's age can be dangerous, with the worst being suicidal tendencies. But Dr. Kaleb said Dr. Donally was one of the best, that if anyone could help Rylie, she could. Toby and Beth agreed that medication would be a last resort.

⁓◦꧁꧂◦⁓

"Mom, do I have to do this? It's bad enough you made me see Dr. Kaleb at school, but why do we have to see this new doctor?" Rylie crossed her arms defiantly as she leaned against the car.

Beth sighed. "Honey, we've talked about this. Dr. Kaleb

recommended that we see this Dr. Donally. "We need to find out what is going on–"

Rylie interrupted, "But I already told you. Nothing is going on."

Beth took her daughter by the hand as they headed towards the building. "Well, something must be. Your grades are slipping, you don't hang out with friends, you sit in your room all the time, and you fight with your sister. You won't talk to your dad or me, so now you can talk to Dr. Donally. Sometimes it is easier for a child to talk to someone outside the family."

Rylie folded her arms across her chest, as stubborn as ever. "Ok. Fine. But I have nothing to talk to her about," Rylie said as she reluctantly allowed her mother to lead her into the building.

Toby poured himself and his wife a cup of coffee and sat down at the kitchen table. It was early December, and Rylie had seen Dr. Donally several times since October.

Beth took a sip of her coffee. Keeping her voice low, so their daughters wouldn't overhear, she said, "Dr. Donally called me and reported the 'Talk Therapy' isn't helping as much as it should she would like."

"Is she making any progress?" Toby asked hopefully.

Beth shrugged. "Dr. Donally said she has opened up a little on some occasions, but other times she refuses to talk. She just sits there staring out the window." Beth circled the rim of her coffee cup with her finger. "She said medication may be the next step, if she can't get Rylie to open up."

Toby took a sip of his coffee. He put his cup down and sighed heavily. "I don't understand how this could happen. How could she change so drastically?"

"I agree. I assumed it was just her being a typical, almost teenager?" Beth questioned. "Hon, I don't want our 12-year-old daughter on meds, especially if they could be dangerous. She's too young."

"Hopefully she'll come out of this or we may not have a choice," Toby said as he sighed.

PARKER BOUNDED down the stairs two at a time and rounded the corner to go into the kitchen but stopped in her tracks when she heard her parent's talking in low voices. It took only seconds for her to realize that they were talking about her sister's therapy sessions. She continued to listen at the door until they finished.

2 - LEXI

Christmas was approaching, and the Shores family were getting ready to make their yearly trip to Oak Canyon Creek, an hour drive from their home in Apache Junction, Arizona.

13-year-old Parker sat down at the kitchen table where her mom was baking Christmas goodies. "Mom, I've been thinking of what we should get Rylie for Christmas," Parker said

"And what might that be?" Beth asked.

"A dog," Parker answered. "She needs a best friend."

Beth raised her eyebrows in surprise.

Parker continued. "I heard you and dad talking about wanting to do more to help her than just the talk therapy sessions with Dr. Donally."

"I don't know, Parker. A dog is a big responsibility. I don't know if she would keep up with the care...she'd have to feed it, walk it every day—"

"I saw a documentary on the Discovery Channel recently

about Emotional Support Dogs. Or other animals that help people who have issues with things like anxiety or depression. I think that's what she needs. It says that these animals help calm people who have these issues." Parker took a breath, then continued. "Maybe one of these could help Rylie."

"Well, maybe we will have to look into this. Let me talk to your father. The decision to get a dog can't be made hastily. It's a big responsibility, a lifelong commitment. It will require a great deal from each of us."

Parker smiled. "I can help her take care of it."

"I admire the way you are trying to find ways to help your sister."

AFTER MUCH DISCUSSION and research on Emotional Support Animals, Toby and Beth had decided that maybe this would help their daughter. Several days later, the family pulled up in front of the animal shelter.

"What are we doing here?" Rylie questioned.

"We have a surprise for you," her sister answered before either of their parents could say a word.

The last one out of the car was Rylie, who was less excited than the rest of her family. Parker grabbed her sister by the hand. "Come on, Ry. This is so awesome! Your first dog."

Rylie pulled away from her sister's grasp. "But I don't want a dog. I don't like dogs. They bite."

"Not all dogs bite, Rylie. Let's just look." Parker grabbed

her hand again, and they followed their parents into the shelter.

They were greeted by a young blonde-haired woman who smiled warmly. "Good morning, folks. What can I do for you?"

Toby smiled. "We are looking for a dog for my youngest daughter."

"I've been reading about emotional support dogs, and my sister needs one," Parker said. "She needs a friend."

The woman smiled down at Rylie. "How exciting for you, young lady. We have many dogs that need a new home to call their own. I'm sure we can find just the right one for you."

Rylie hid behind her sister as they followed the lady into the kennel area. They were greeted by barking and wagging tails. It seemed all the dogs were begging to be chosen. As they listened to the lady tell each dog's story, Rylie cowered behind her sister.

Parker stopped in front of a kennel housing a large German Shepherd. "This one is beautiful."

"This is Shasta. She's about three years old. Very gentle." Rylie stared at the big dog. *She's too big, Rylie thought to herself. Big dogs bite and jump on people. I need to get out of here.* While her family continued to admire Shasta, she continued walking down the row of kennels, looking for the nearest way out. She rounded the corner to another row of kennels and stopped, glancing around for a door that would take her away from these dogs.

As she glanced around, her eyes came to rest on a small dog huddled in the corner of a kennel. She slowly approached the kennel. The little dog remained still.

"Here you are," Parker said as she rounded the corner. "I FOUND HER!" Parker yelled loud enough for the others to hear. She stopped beside her sister and looked at the little dog that seemed to have Rylie mesmerized.

The blonde woman smiled as she and Beth and Toby came alongside the girls. "This is Lexi. She's only been here a couple of weeks. She is a 1-year-old Yorkie. Would you like to meet her?"

Rylie nodded shyly. The woman unlocked the kennel and took Rylie by the hand, leading her into the kennel. "You can sit down on the floor beside her if you'd like."

Rylie did as the lady suggested.

"Ok... reach out and gently pet her."

Before Rylie could pet her, Lexi climbed into her lap and began licking her arm. The smile on Rylie's face was priceless.

The woman smiled. "I think she picked you."

"What do you think, sweetheart?" Beth asked her daughter.

"I want her," Rylie said softly.

Parker smiled. "She is gorgeous, Rylie. You made a good choice."

Rylie stood up, holding her new dog gently in her arms.

"Are you going to change her name or keep Lexi?" Parker asked.

Rylie was thoughtful for a moment. "I like her name, Lexi."

"Welcome to the family, little girl," Parker said as she patted the top of Lexi's head. "She gets to go to the cabin with us, doesn't she?"

"Of course," Toby answered. "She's part of the family now. Where we go, she goes."

A short while later, after the paperwork was completed, and the adoption fee paid, the family took their new member out to the car. Rylie held her new friend carefully, gently petting her. Lexi settled down and fell asleep in her lap.

"Looks like they were made for each other," Parker commented.

Beth turned to look at her daughters. "I think you are right, Park." The smile on Rylie's face told Beth that they had made the right decision in getting a dog for their young daughter. *She was definitely attracted to Lexi the moment she saw her. And Lexi had gone right to her. Yes, this match was meant to be.*

3 - LEXI

$\mathcal{B}$y the time the family left for the cabin, Lexi sported a harness declaring her an official Emotional Support Animal. In just a week, Beth and Toby had noticed a change in their youngest daughter. She had begun to spend time outside running with her new best friend, playing tug of war, laughing, and often could be found just sitting on the grass with Lexi lying in her lap. A match made in heaven, Parker had called it.

They arrived at the cabin, and Rylie and Lexi were the first out of the car. Parker shook her head. "Is that my sister?" She laughed. Watching the changes in her sister since bringing Lexi home had been amazing. The two had bonded immediately. *But what happens when we go back to school?* Parker thought to herself.

LATER THAT NIGHT, Parker slipped out of bed and quietly made her way to the living room to find her parents reading. "Mom and Dad?"

Beth put down the book she was reading. Toby did the same. "Sweetheart, what are you doing up at this hour? You should be asleep," Beth said.

"I've been thinking.," Parker answered. "Will Rylie be able to take Lexi to school? She's been doing great at home, but when we go back to school, she may still be her old self. She doesn't interact much with other kids. I've heard kids comment that she is snobbish or stuck up because she won't talk to anyone."

Toby was thoughtful for a moment. "Well, I'm not sure she will be able to. They may see it as a distraction to the other children. But after the holidays, I will call the school and see if something can be worked out. How does that sound?"

"Okay, Dad." Parker yawned. "I'm going back to bed."

"Night, sweetheart," Beth said as her daughter went back to her bedroom.

DECEMBER 23RD, the family gathered around the fire pit to roast marshmallows and sing Christmas carols, accompanied by Toby on the guitar. It was a cool, crisp Arizona evening. Rylie sat cross-legged on the ground with Lexi lying in her lap. After several minutes of singing and laughing with her family, Rylie picked up Lexi's leash and headed towards the cabin. Suddenly, and without warning, Lexi began barking, then started running. Caught off guard, Lexi yanked the leash out of Rylie's hand. She started running to catch up with Lexi.

Rylie suddenly stopped dead in her tracks, then let out a blood-curdling scream. She saw a coyote, holding Lexi in its mouth, trying to drag her away, but the leash was snagged on a bush.

Toby dropped his guitar and took off running in the direction of the screams, followed by Beth and Parker. Toby put out his arm to stop his wife and daughter. He picked up a rock and yelled as he threw it at the coyote that stood only a few feet away. The coyote dropped the small dog, turned, and ran into the woods. Toby and Beth ran towards Lexi, while Parker hurried over to her little sister, who was crying hysterically.

Toby knelt down beside the Lexi and gently touched her as he scanned her for injuries. He saw puncture wounds, oozing with blood.

"She's still alive, but there's a lot of blood," he said as he gently lifted her. "We need to get her to the vet. Get a blanket." *This doesn't look good,* Toby told himself. *She is so tiny, and this bite looks deep. Come on, little girl, hang on.*

Beth hurried into the cabin, returning seconds later. With Toby's help, she carefully wrapped Lexi in the blanket, then hurried her daughters to the car for the 20-minute ride into town to the Oak Creek Canyon Animal Hospital.

4 - LEXI

The ride to the hospital seemed to take forever, but they finally arrived. Toby carried Lexi while the rest of the family followed. They were met at the door by the Vet Assistant.

"What happened?" She asked as she took Lexi into her arms.

"Coyote attack," Toby answered. "It had her, but the leash got caught on a bush, thank god, or I'm sure she'd be gone. It dropped her when I threw a rock at it."

"We'll do our best. You can wait in there," she said, nodding towards the room off to the right, then carried Lexi through the double doors at the end of the hallway.

"It's all my fault," Rylie said through her tears. "It's my fault. It's my fault."

Beth put her arms around her, speaking softly. "It wasn't your fault, honey. It was a coyote. That's what they do. They attack other animals. There was nothing you could do. We're just thankful you are okay."

"But I let go of the leash," Rylie protested. "If I hadn't, Lexi wouldn't have run to the coyote."

"But then he may have gotten you," Parker said.

Toby put his arms around Rylie. "Coyotes aren't known to attack humans. But small dogs tend to think they are bigger than they are, so in Lexi's eyes, she was protecting you from danger. She's a brave little girl."

"Yes, she is." Beth agreed. Rylie pulled away from her father's arms and ran over to the corner of the room, sinking down to the floor. She brought her knees up and wrapped her arms around them as sobs shook her tiny body.

Beth looked helplessly at her husband. Toby shrugged and shook his head. He couldn't find words to comfort his daughter. He knew it didn't look good for Lexi, and he didn't want to give his child false hope that she would pull through the vicious attack.

The next few hours passed slowly for the waiting family. The only sound was the loud ticking of the clock. Rylie had cried herself to sleep, still huddled in the corner. Parker sat on the floor beside her, while their parents sat silently in nearby chairs.

"Mr. And Mrs. Shores?"

Rylie woke with a start, then quickly stood up when she saw the doctor.

"How is my dog?" Rylie asked quickly. "Is she okay?"

"I'm Dr. Braddock. It was touch and go for a while, as the wounds were quite deep, and she did lose a fair amount of blood. But she is a fighter. She is stable now, but I would like to keep her here tonight for observation, "

Toby nodded. "Yes, I think that would be best.

Rylie looked at her dad, then Dr. Braddock. "She can't go home with me?"

Beth shook her head. "Not tonight, honey. Dr. Braddock needs to keep an eye on her to make sure she will be okay. You want what's best for Lexi, don't you?"

Rylie nodded. "Yes. You'll take good care of her?" She questioned.

Dr. Braddock smiled. "Yes, young lady. We will take very good care of her."

"Okay, then," Rylie said softly. "We'll come back first thing in the morning. Right, Dad?"

"Of course, we will," Toby answered. "Thank you, Dr. Braddock." He shook the doctor's hand, then ushered his family outside to the car. It had been a long evening, and they were all tired.

The ride home was quiet, as each was lost in their own thoughts. Beth glanced at her daughters in the back seat. It was only two days until Christmas. *Wil little Lexi survive this attack?* She closed her eyes in silent prayer, glad the car was dark so no one could see her tears. She was praying for a Christmas miracle.

***

"CAN WE GO SEE LEXI NOW?" Rylie ran into the kitchen the next morning. Beth was preparing breakfast; Toby was sipping a hot cup of coffee.

"After breakfast, young lady," Toby said as he put his coffee cup down.

Rylie sat down at her place at the table. "Can we please hurry? She isn't used to being alone."

Before anyone could answer, the phone rang. Toby answered it quickly. By now, Parker had joined her sister at the table.

Toby hung up the phone, then turned to face his family. "That was Dr. Braddock."

Beth turned away from the stove, waiting for her husband to continue. She searched his face, fearing the worst. *Please say she is going to be okay,* she whispered softly to herself.

"Lexi made it through the night with flying colors and is going to be okay. We can pick her up later this morning. He said she is a real fighter."

Beth smiled, relieved. We got our Christmas miracle!

Parker took a bite of her egg. "I'm glad Lexi is going to be okay. Come on, Ry. Let's get ready to go."

Beth placed a hand on each daughter's shoulder. "Let's finish breakfast so we can go bring our girl home."

The girls nodded as they continued eating their breakfast, anxious to finish so they could go pick up little Lexi.

5 - LEXI

$\mathcal{T}$he holidays were over, and it was back to school.

Toby called the school principal and explained the situation. Mrs. Koskie was understanding and had agreed to try it today to see how it would go. She suggested that Rylie talk to the class about Lexi and the role she played as an emotional support animal. She had also suggested that Beth accompany Rylie and Lexi to school. Toby had agreed.

After hanging up with Mrs. Koskie, Toby turned to Rylie. She listened carefully as her dad explained what she would need to do if she brought Lexi to school. She shook her head. "Dad, I can't do this. I can't...I can't get up and talk in front of all those kids. They'll laugh at me."

Toby put his arm around her. "Honey, no one is going to laugh at you. I think they will be interested to learn about Lexi. I agreed with Mrs. Koskie that you would share with the class what Lexi does for you as your emotional support dog. I know it won't be easy, but I want you to promise me that you will give it your best. Can you do that for me?"

Rylie nodded slowly. "I'll try, Dad."

Toby gave her a hug. "That's my girl."

BETH PARKED at the school later that morning. It had been decided that she would sit in Rylie's classroom for a bit to help her daughter with Lexi if needed.

Rylie held Lexi close as she carried her into her classroom with Beth close behind her.

Her teacher, Mrs. Jeremy, greeted her at the door. "Welcome back, Rylie. Hello, Mrs. Shores. And this must be our new student," She gently patted Lexi on the head. "Mrs. Koskie explained the situation, and I think having Lexi here will be good for Rylie, and the other children as well. What a darling she is. I thought you could introduce her first thing as soon as everyone takes their seats."

"I don't know what to say," Rylie said quietly.

Her teacher smiled. "Just tell them about Lexi, like what an emotional support dog does for you…anything you might want them to know about her."

Rylie nodded, unable to speak around the lump in her throat.

Mrs. Jeremy patted her on the shoulder. "You will do fine, Rylie."

She turned her attention to the class. "Ok, everyone, take your seats. We have a special guest this morning. Rylie Shores would like to introduce you to her friend Lexi."

Beth glanced at the students as she heard the snickers

from several of the boys in the back of the room. Rylie carried Lexi to the front of the classroom.

"This is Lexi," Rylie started softly. "She is a one-year-old Yorkie. I got her for Christmas. She is my Emotional Support Dog." She looked at her mother, her eyes pleading for help. She didn't know what else to say.

Beth smiled, sensing her daughter's discomfort. "Tell them what an emotional support animal is."

Rylie nodded. "She is calm and helps me when I am nervous or anxious. An Emotional Support Animal can be other animals, too, not just dogs."

"That's wonderful, Rylie. What else can you tell us about Lexi?"

Rylie looked at her mother for assistance.

Beth smiled as she stood beside her daughter. "Emotional Support dogs are dogs that provide comfort and support in forms of affection and companionship for a person suffering from various emotional conditions, such as the anxiety Rylie has in social situations. These dogs aren't required to perform certain tasks like service dogs are. Lexi comforts Rylie when she is feeling anxious or scared."

A girl in the front row raised her hand.

"Do you have a question, Lilly?" Mrs. Jeremy asked.

"Can we pet her?" Lilly asked.

"Yes, you sure may," Beth answered. "This little girl loves attention."

"I would like everyone to get in a circle. If it is ok with Rylie, we will put Lexi in the middle, and everyone will get a chance to pet her." Mrs. Jeremy looked at Rylie. "Would this be okay?"

"Yes, Ma'am," Rylie answered as the class formed a circle and sat down on the floor. Rylie found a place in the circle and sat down as she sat Lexi down in the center of the circle. Lexi excitedly ran around to several of the children, giving several of them puppy dog kisses. The children laughed as Lexi ran around the circle.

Beth felt tears come into her eyes as she watched her daughter laugh with her classmates.

"Thank you for bringing her, Rylie," Lilly said. She looked up at Mrs. Jeremy. "Can she bring Lexi every day, Mrs. Jeremy?"

The teacher smiled. "We will see. I will need to check with Mrs. Koskie." Mrs. Jeremy left the circle and joined Beth a short distance away. "This little dog has done wonders for Rylie, Mrs. Shores."

Beth nodded in agreement. "Yes, she has. At home, she doesn't isolate herself in her room anymore. She loves spending time outside playing with Lexi. She is focused on taking care of her. "

"I feel confident that in time we will see changes in her here at school as well," Mrs. Jeremy stated.

Beth nodded. Dr. Donally is pleased with her progress too. We meet with her as a family next week to discuss whether or not Rylie will still need to continue seeing her.

"We've never had an animal allowed to come to school with a student, but like they say, there's a first time for everything. In this case, I believe it would be in Rylie's best interest. I will speak with Mrs. Koskie this afternoon and get back to you soon."

"Thank you, Mrs. Jeremy. I will be looking forward to

hearing from you." Beth shook the teacher's hand, then went over to the circle and knelt beside her daughter. "Time for Lexi to go home, Ry." Rylie picked up her dog and gave her a hug, then handed her to her mother.

"Bye, Lexi. "A chorus of bye-byes rang out in unison from the children.

"Okay, class. Let's take our seats." Mrs. Jeremy said with a smile. "Maybe you could all thank Rylie for sharing Lexi with us."

"Thanks, Rylie." Lilly was the first to speak. "She is a neat dog. I hope you can bring her again."

"I hope so too," Rylie said quietly, feeling relieved that she had been able to speak in front of the class, and glad that it was over.

As the children started to take their seats, Mrs. Jeremy looked around the room. Her gaze settled on Rylie. The child seemed to have a different look about her. A look of contentment. It was obvious to her that the little rescue dog had definitely brought changes to the life of this child. She smiled to herself as a thought occurred to her, *Did Rylie rescue Lexi, or did Lexi rescue Rylie?*

Maybe a little of both, she thought to herself as she sat down at her desk.

THAT EVENING AT SUPPER, Rylie excitedly shared her day with Toby and Parker. Beth couldn't help but smile at her daughter's excitement.

"It was awesome, Toby. I've never seen her like this. She

was laughing and interacting with the other kids. All because of a little dog. Mrs. Jeremy is going to see about letting her bring Lexi every day. But we shouldn't let our hopes get up too high."

Before Toby could answer, the phone rang. "I'll get it," Parker said as she jumped up from her chair and ran into the living room, returning seconds later. "Mom, it's for you. Mrs. Jeremy."

Beth excused herself and went to take the call. She returned to the table a few minutes later, smiling. "Good news." She said as she sat down. "Mrs. Jeremy talked to the principal, and they made the decision to allow Rylie to bring Lexi on a trial basis this week to see how it goes. If all goes well, they will consider allowing her to bring her every day."

"I can bring Lexi to school?" Rylie questioned; not sure she had heard right. Beth nodded.

"Yes, you can bring her. But there will be rules you will need to follow. And you still need to continue the therapy until the Dr. says otherwise."

Rylie nodded. "I promise to follow them, and I will do the therapy. I want to be able to keep bringing her. May I be excused? I wanna go tell Lexi." Without waiting for an answer, Rylie jumped up from the table and ran into the living room, where Lexi was sleeping on her doggy couch.

Parker watched her sister in amazement. "Wow. I've never seen her like this."

Beth smiled. "You should have seen her today. Between the therapy and Lexi, she is like a totally different girl."

"Getting Lexi was definitely the right thing to do," Toby

stated. "And Parker, we owe that to you, it was your idea. Rylie is so lucky to have you as her big sister."

Parker smiled. "It's my job to watch out for her. She's my baby sister. I want her to be happy, and I hated seeing other kids tease her."

Beth reached across the table and grabbed Toby's hand. "We are so very fortunate to have two wonderful daughters,"

Toby nodded. "Yes, we are."

Parker started to laugh as she said, "You have three daughters-Me, Rylie, and LEXI!"

Beth and Toby joined in the laughter.

With the help of a small Yorkie, their young daughter would be ok; they were all sure of that. Rylie had a best friend.

THE END

STORY FIVE

Sarah's Song

1 - SARAH'S SONG

*H*annah *slowly opened the door to the nursery. A shiver ran down her spine as she glanced around the room. Everything was exactly as she had left it. As her eyes came to rest upon the large portrait on the wall above the dresser, memories came flooding back to her.*

"Can't you do anything?" Josh pleaded.

"It's too risky," Dr. Hampton replied. "The baby is in distress. The ultrasound shows that the cord is wrapped around her neck. To be honest, Mr. Bryton, although the baby is about two months premature, its chances are good–– better than if we try to delay delivery."

"What about Hannah? Is it better for her, too?"

"Yes."

Josh sighed, reluctantly accepting the Dr.'s advice, and giving him permission to do the procedure.

Dr. Hampton quickly ordered Hannah be prepped for an emergency C-Section. There was no way to know how long the baby may have been without oxygen, and the only way to save her was to deliver her immediately.

"It's a girl!" He announced, passing the tiny infant to a nurse.

"Is she alright?" Hannah gasped weakly, as she listened for a sound from the newborn.

"We'll know in a few minutes, but she's breathing on her own."

Exhausted, Hannah fell back against the pillows.

Josh leaned over and placed a soft kiss on her lips. "We've got a daughter, darling. Happy?"

"Very," Hannah whispered quietly as she closed her eyes. "What time is it?"

Josh looked at the clock on the wall. "2:45 AM."

Hannah opened her eyes, speaking softly. "Happy birthday, sweetheart. I guess I gave you your present after all."

Josh kissed her again. "You sure did. And she is the best present you could ever have given me."

Dr. Hampton smiled at the proud new parents. "Congratulations. Mrs. Bryton, we're going to take you to a room. You've had a long night. Mr. Bryton, I think it would be a good idea for you to go home and get some rest also."

"Can't we even see our baby?" Hannah asked.

"Premature infants need immediate care. They'll tend to her in the neonatal intensive care unit and make sure that there are no problems. You'll be able to see her later this afternoon or early this evening."

JOSH ENTERED Hannah's hospital room later that afternoon, a bouquet of red roses held behind his back. He greeted her with a kiss. "Hi, mom." He handed her the roses.

"Oh, Josh. They're beautiful."

"Beautiful roses for a beautiful lady. Our parents are very excited about their new granddaughter." Josh said with a smile.

"Have you seen her yet?" Hannah asked wearily

"I stopped by the NICU before coming in here. She is a beautiful little princess. Haven't you seen her?" Josh questioned, raising his eyebrows.

"No, she's too small to be taken out of her incubator, and they won't let me get up yet. Did you call Mr. and Mrs. Whitney? Hannah asked, referring to their boss and his wife.

"I sure did. They were just as thrilled and excited as we are. You'd think our new daughter was *their* very own granddaughter." Josh replied.

A moment later, the door opened, and Dr. Hampton came in. "I'm glad you're both here because there's something I have to talk to you about."

Josh and Hannah looked at each other, then back at Dr. Hampton. "Is something wrong with the baby?" Josh asked.

Dr. Hampton nodded slowly. "I'm afraid there is. She has developed respiratory distress syndrome. RDS is very common in premature infants."

"What exactly is it?" Hannah managed to ask.

"The infant's breathing appears to be normal at birth but

begins to have grunting respirations within a few hours. The baby starts using abdominal muscles to help her breathe, but the lungs don't expand properly. She needs extra oxygen and has to be ventilated artificially. We put her on a respirator."

"Will our baby be okay? I mean, will she live?"

"I promise that we'll do everything in our power for her."

"She's in God's hands," Josh said softly as the doctor left the room. They prayed together for their new daughter.

LATER THAT NIGHT, after Josh left to go home, Hannah lay awake, thinking about their new baby girl. She was so tiny and fragile. She had cried when she heard she would be hooked up to a machine that would help her to breathe.

Josh had tried to hide it, but she had seen tears well up in his eyes. During their six years of marriage, she had never seen her husband cry. They had waited three years for this child. *Would they lose her now?*

Hannah turned on the light and picked up her Bible from the table beside the bed. She opened it to the book of Genesis and read the story of Abraham, Sarah, and Isaac. Abraham and Sarah had waited so long for a child, and God had given them Isaac, even in their old age. Isaac had brought his parent's so much joy, just as their new daughter had brought to them.

Because she was premature, they hadn't yet been thinking of names. Hannah remembered how Josh had said that she looked like a beautiful little princess.

Her mind wandered back to her own childhood. She remembered a book called "A Little Princess." It was about a little girl named Sarah, called Princess, because the name means princess. Hannah smiled to herself. *Sarah will be a perfect name for our baby. Now, what could her middle name be? It must be something special too.*

She reached over and picked up the name book from the nightstand. She leafed through it, hoping something would catch her eye. She thought about different names. *It should be something that describes the joy that she has brought to us.* Hannah smiled and said out loud, "Sarah Joy Bryton." Hannah found the name in the book, again reading aloud. "Joy— joyful one." As she looked down the page, another name caught her eye. "Joylynn— overflowing joy. *Sarah Joylynn Bryton*, a beautiful name," she said as she drifted off to sleep.

FOUR DAYS LATER, Hannah was scheduled to be released from the hospital. She awoke early, anxious to go home, but not wanting to leave little Sarah behind. Unable to stay in bed any longer, Hannah put her robe on and walked down to the NICU.

"I thought I might find you here."

Hannah turned to see Josh standing beside her with a big smile on his face. "What are you doing here so early? I thought you weren't coming until lunchtime."

"I couldn't wait any longer. I asked Mr. Whitney if I could

have the morning off so I could take you home. He graciously gave me the day off. He said you shouldn't be alone on your first day home. And I agree." Josh said, still smiling.

"So do I," Hannah answered. "But I wish Sarah could go home with us. I don't want to leave her."

"I know, but she'll be getting excellent care while she's here. The Dr. said she'll be able to go home when she starts breathing on her own and gains a little weight."

As the young couple gazed lovingly at their newborn daughter, they didn't see Dr. Hampton approach them until he spoke. "Excuse me, Mr. and Mrs. Bryton. I need to talk to you for a few minutes. Let's go down to your room." Josh and Hannah looked at each other, then followed him down the hall. Once they were all seated, Dr. Hampton spoke. "During the past few days, Sarah's breathing has improved slightly, but we have found other problems. Her lactose enzyme is insufficient, so milk is not digested properly, and she isn't gaining weight. Her immune system is not fully developed, so she is very susceptible to respiratory disorders. We also suspect anoxia, which means insufficient oxygen during delivery."

"T-that could cause brain damage, couldn't it?" Josh asked.

"I'm afraid so. But it may be several days or even weeks before we know if she has suffered brain damage. Sarah was born two months early. She's very lucky to be alive."

"Dr. Hampton, would it be okay for Hannah and I to be alone for a little while?" Dr. Hampton nodded and left the room, understanding how the new parents needed to work through their feelings together about having a very ill child.

"My biggest dream for my life was to get married and have a family," Hannah said softly. "I've always wanted to have a child of my own. But I never thought that something could be wrong with her. Josh, I don't want to lose our baby."

"We won't lose her, honey. She is in God's hands. We'll put our trust in him."

Hannah was silent as she fought back her tears. "I'm scared, Josh. Really scared," she said after several minutes. "I-I'm so afraid that she'll— that she'll die. If she dies… " Hannah's voice trailed off as Josh put his arms around her.

"Don't think that. Come on, let's go home."

"Can we stop at the NICU once more before we go?"

"Of course, we can. We'll say a special prayer for her before we go." Josh picked up Hannah's suitcase and followed her from the room.

At the NICU, Hannah gently touched the window that separated them from their daughter, wondering if they would ever be able to hold her or even touch her.

Lord, please take care of our baby girl, Hannah prayed silently as she reached for her husband's hand.

Then, out loud, she continued…

"Please guide the doctors as they care for her. We know that she is in your hands. Thank you, heavenly father, for allowing us to be parents of your very special child; we thank you for what you will do in her life. Amen."

Hannah looked over Josh, smiling faintly. "She really will be okay, won't she?"

Josh squeezed her hand. "Yes, our baby will be okay. Are you ready to go?"

Hannah nodded, "I'm ready now."

Josh and Hannah both whispered goodbye to little Sarah and headed towards the elevator.

2 - SARAH'S SONG

*J*osh glanced across the table at Hannah, who only picked at her food. Her mind seemed to be millions of miles away. "Aren't you going to eat, Sweetheart?"

"I'm sorry. You fixed the terrific meal, but I'm not very hungry right now. Is it okay with you if I go upstairs and lay down for a while? I'm kinda tired."

"Of course, it's okay. You go ahead, and I'll clean up the kitchen. We can warm your plate up later when you feel like eating."

Hannah forced a smile. "Thanks."

Josh watched as Hannah left the kitchen. He knew what was on her mind. Their baby daughter might never be the healthy child that they had longed for.

Josh got up and begin clearing the table, but then changed his mind. The kitchen could wait until later. He went up to the bedroom. Hannah was lying on the bed, staring at the ceiling. Tears were streaming down her cheeks. Josh sat down beside her. "Are you okay?"

"Yeah, sure. I just wish Sarah was."

"Sarah will be fine."

"But she may have brain damage."

Josh rubbed her cheek. "Honey, Sarah is our daughter. We have been waiting for her for three years."

"For three years, we prayed for a child. I wanted you to have a child that you could be proud of. Why was she born this way, instead of being healthy? What are we going to tell our families and friends?"

Josh thought to himself, *I have to be strong for her.* "We'll tell them that we have a very special daughter. We have a beautiful baby girl named Sarah Joylynn Bryton, and we love her."

When Hannah didn't say anything, Josh continued, "She's the child we've been waiting for."

Hannah shook her head. "No, she's not. We were waiting for a healthy baby. Sarah may be handicapped. You heard what Dr. Hampton said. She may never be like other children. I'm sorry, Josh. I don't know how much—"

"Honey, enough already!" Josh interrupted. "You are not responsible for any of this. Stop blaming yourself. Are we not going to love her just because she is handicapped?"

"Josh, I don't— oh, never mind," Hannah said.

Happy to change the subject, Josh said. "I've got some errands to do in town. Do you want to go?"

"No. I'd like to be alone for a while. You go ahead."

Josh gave her a quick kiss on the cheek. "I'll see you later."

AFTER HE HAD GONE, Hannah thought about their relationship over the past six years. They had met while spending the summer singing with the gospel music group from the college that they both attended. Shortly after their marriage, right after college, they were offered a chance to audition for the Lance Whitney show. Featuring gospel music, short skits about Biblical events, and witnessing for the Lord, it was a fantastic opportunity to do professionally what they both loved. They spent a couple of weeks practicing together and were finally ready. After getting hired for the show, they would spend most weekdays at the studio rehearsing, and on most weekends, the show would tour in neighboring states. Often, they would do an extended month-long tour, traveling as far as the opposite coast. As a result, Josh and Hannah had only an occasional day off, but they didn't mind, as they loved the job.

After their third anniversary, still trying, but not getting any results, they went to a specialist to find out why they couldn't conceive. They were told that there didn't seem to be any medical reason, and they should keep trying.

And now, after three years of patience and prayers, they finally had a child. But for how long? Hannah asked herself.

JOSH PARKED the car in front of Lance's Whitney's house. He felt the need to talk to someone other than Hannah, and he hoped that Mr. Whitney was home. He rang the doorbell and waited.

Emilie Whitney opened the door. "Hi, Josh. Come on in. What brings you here?"

"If you not busy, I like to talk to you and Mr. Whitney."

"Come on into the living room." Josh followed her in.

Lance looked up and smiled. "Hi, Josh. How are the new parents?"

"I wish I could say we're okay," Josh said, shrugging his shoulders. "But we're struggling."

"What are you talking about? Is something wrong?"

Josh nodded, then told them what they had been told by Dr. Hampton.

"How did Hannah take it?" Emilie asked.

"All day she's been acting as though Sarah died. She's blaming herself. She thinks that maybe she did things during her pregnancy that caused her to go into premature labor and caused Sarah to have so many problems. She says that she loves Sarah, but I don't think it's coming from the heart. I think she's upset because she knows that she has to love her own baby."

"That doesn't sound like something she would do. Josh, I'm sure she loves the baby." Lance said.

"Maybe I'm wrong, but I don't think she's being honest with me about how she really feels. It sounds like she's just saying a bunch of words with no true meaning."

Emilie lightly touched Joshes' arm. "Josh, would you like me to talk to her? Sometimes another woman can under-stand these things a little better."

"Thank you, Mrs. Whitney. Maybe she'll be a little more honest with you."

"I'll go over tomorrow while you're at the studio. Josh," Emilie said with a reassuring smile. I'm sure everything will be okay.

"Sarah is a beautiful baby," Lance said. "I know it will be hard for you both to accept that she may be disabled. But you must remember to be thankful that she is still with us."

"I guess we had such big dreams for her that we didn't even consider the possibility that something could be wrong with her." Josh looked down at his feet. "Mr. and Mrs. Whitney, will you please pray for us? I'm trying to be strong, but…well, I hate to admit it, but sometimes I wonder too. Will we be able to handle it? Will God give us the strength to handle whatever comes our way?"

Emilie gave him a hug. "Of course, I will pray for you. And Josh, remember that you're never alone. The Lord is always with you, and he knows the desires of your heart even before you do. Sarah is a very special child of God, and he has chosen you and Hannah to be her very special parents. He will help you to handle it. Put your trust in him."

Josh looked up at Mrs. Whitney and said, "Thank you. I better get going. I told Hannah that I wouldn't be gone very long. I'll see you tomorrow." Josh thanked them again, then hurried outside, feeling a little better. Still, he couldn't help but wonder to himself, *why Lord would you give us this burden?*

THE NEXT AFTERNOON while Josh was at the studio, Hannah spent most of the morning doing the laundry and was now putting the clothes away. Josh told her to spend the day resting, but she felt the need to be busy. She was in the bedroom, changing the sheets on the bed when the doorbell rang. She groaned. *Who could that be? I really don't feel like talking to anyone,* she thought as she went downstairs. Opening the door, she was surprised it was Mrs. Whitney. "Hi, Mrs. Whitney."

"Hello, Hannah. Did I interrupt anything?"

Trying to be polite, she replied, "Nothing really. I was just finishing the laundry. It really piled up while I was in the hospital. Would you like some coffee?"

"That would be nice. Thank you." Emilie followed her into the kitchen and sat down at the table.

Hannah poured 2 cups of coffee. Neither of them spoke until Hannah was seated at the table, then Emilie asked, "How are you doing, Hannah?"

"I'm fine. I still get tired easily, but I'm okay." Hannah answered.

"Hannah, last night, Josh came over to our house. He told us about Sarah's problems. He's worried that you don't love her." Emilie said softly

"Of course, I love her! She's my baby. Why would he say that?"

Emilie told her what Josh had said, then asked, "Is there anything else bothering you?" Hannah was silent for a moment as tears filled her eyes. Emilie noticed a sudden change and become concerned. "What is it, Hannah?"

"I'm scared, Mrs. Whitney. I'm afraid that I won't be a

good mother to her, that I won't be able to take proper care of her. It's likely she'll always require special care, and I don't know if I can give it to her." Hannah paused, took a deep breath, then let it out before continuing. "I wanted to give Josh a child that he could be proud of. Did I do something to cause this?"

"Of course not, dear." Emilie put her arms around Hannah as she cried.

Sobs shook her entire body. "I just don't know if I can do it."

Everything will be fine," she said soothingly. "You'll be a wonderful mother to your daughter. And you're not alone. You have Josh. And the Lord will help you. Just ask him. In fact, let's pray now." Mrs. Whitney held Hannah's hand and bowed her head.

Hannah half listened, as she was wondering, why God would you give us a handicapped child?

When she was finished, Mrs. Whitney asked, "Are you feeling better?"

Hannah answered, "I do. Thank you." She really wasn't but didn't want to worry, Mrs. Whitney. She couldn't get it out of her head that God gave them a handicapped child.

⚜

EMILIE WALKED into the studio a short time later. Lance greeted her with a kiss. "Hi, honey."

"Hi. I came to talk to Josh. I just left Hannah."

"I'll get him, and we can go into the office." With that,

Lance headed towards the dressing rooms. The drummer in the act, Jake, answered the knock on the door.

"Is Josh in here?"

Jake nodded and called Josh, who was just coming out of the bathroom.

"Josh, will you please come into the office for a few minutes?"

"Sure, Mr. Whitney." Josh followed him into the office and saw Mrs. Whitney. "Hi, Mrs. Whitney."

"Hello, Josh," Emilie said. "I just left your house."

"Did you find out anything?"

"Josh, I believe that Hannah loves Sarah but--"

"Then why does she act as though she's ashamed of her? That doesn't sound like love to me. She sounds like she's afraid to tell her friends and family that we have a handicapped child. Does that sound like love to you?"

"Josh, Hannah is very scared. She— "

Josh interrupted her again. "Scared? I don't understand. Of what?"

"Her fear is real to her. She's afraid that she won't be able to be a good mother to Sarah. Or give her the special care that she'll always require. She's afraid of failing."

"I-I guess I didn't realize what she was feeling. What can I do to help her?"

"She doesn't think you will understand. Josh, you need to show her that you do understand how she feels."

"How do I do that?"

"This is your first baby. Being a parent is a big responsibility and having a handicapped child doesn't make it any easier. You have to work together. And that means you have to have open and honest communication. Don't keep your feelings inside. Share them with each other. Instead of thinking of her as a handicapped child, consider her a very special blessing. God has chosen you and Hannah to be her parents. He would not have given her to you if you couldn't handle it."

"I guess I never thought of it like that. Thank you. I'll talk to her when I get home."

Emilie put her hand on Josh's arm. "Josh, Sarah is a very lucky little girl. You and Hannah have so much love to give to her. And to each other."

After the Whitney's left the room, Josh thought about their conversation, which made sense, but still couldn't help wondering why God thought they were the ones who should take on this burden. *Why did our first child have to be born like this?*

3 - SARAH'S SONG

*W*hen josh got home from work that evening, he found Hannah in the kitchen preparing supper. "Hi, babe."

"Hi." She didn't turn around as she stirred the food.

"Mrs. Whitney stopped by the studio after she left here. Hannah, we need to talk."

"Let's wait until after supper," Hannah said. "Besides, I don't think there's much to discuss."

Josh insisted. "Yes, there is. I think we need to talk about how we feel about Sarah."

Suddenly seething with anger, Hannah slammed the pan down on the burner with a bang. "I don't care what you think! I don't feel like talking about it right now!" She turned to face him and could see the hurt look on his face as he stood there. Relenting, she continued, "Alright, fine. If you want to talk now...let's talk."

Josh was shocked. She had never spoken to him like that.

"No…you're right. Let's eat first. We'll sit and talk after supper. I'll go upstairs and get washed up."

Hannah nodded as he left the room.

A few minutes later, they were seated at the table and bowed their heads in prayer. Josh felt he had to do his best to be strong for Hannah, even if he might have his own doubts. He took a breath and bowed his head, and prayed…

"Dear heavenly Father, we thank you for this nice day that you have given us. Please be with our little Sarah and strengthen her tiny body. Lord, please be with us and show us how to care for her. Give us the strength we need and prepare our hearts for whatever may come our way. Thank you for this food and bless it to our body's use. Amen."

Josh looked over at Hannah. Tears were starting to form, and he could tell that she was trying hard not to cry. He reached over and touched her hand. "Are you okay? Don't be afraid to cry. I know how much it hurts."

The angry thoughts she had earlier subsided into a dull headache that was starting to form. "I'm not very hungry. I'd like to go upstairs and lie down. I'm tired."

"Sure," Josh said softly as he gently squeezed her hand. "I'll put the food away."

She nodded, then wearily made her way upstairs. She wished she had something stronger to take for the headache, but Josh was firmly against anything other than aspirin.

Josh stared after her, worried. Since arriving home from the hospital, the day before, she had hardly eaten at all, and last night she had been restless, waking up several times during the night. She still seemed to tire easily, and he was afraid that if she didn't start eating and getting some rest, she would make herself sick and end up back in the hospital.

After doing the dishes and cleaning the kitchen, Josh went to their bedroom. Hannah was lying in bed, staring at the ceiling. Her hands were folded across her stomach, and he could see her pale cheeks were now wet. Josh sat down on the bed beside her. As gently as he could, he said, "Still want to talk?"

Hannah looked up at him. "I keep hoping that this is all a bad dream, and when I wake up, we'll have a healthy daughter, and she won't be in the hospital. She'll be at home with us. Pretty silly, huh?"

Josh focused and tried his best to remember the way Mrs. Whitney had tried to comfort him as he said, "It's not silly at all. I know she's not exactly the healthy child of our dreams, but Mrs. Whitney said that we must remember to thank the Lord that he allowed her to live. He could've taken her a few months ago when you got so sick and were rushed to the hospital. But he didn't. If God chose us, he must know that we can do it." *Please, God, let me be right about that,* he thought to himself.

Hannah sighed and said, "I do love our baby. I love her very much." She sat up and put her arms around him. "I love you very much too. Sorry I was so angry earlier."

With a sigh of relief, Josh said, "I love you too," as he kissed her.

HANNAH WOKE up later that night and looked at the clock on the nightstand beside the bed. 12:45 AM. *Where is he?* she wondered as she noticed the empty bed beside her. She got up and put her robe on, thinking maybe he went to the kitchen for a bite to eat. As she opened the door to the bedroom, she noticed a light on in Sarah's room down the hall. "Josh?" Hannah said, entering the room. "What are you doing in here?"

"Just thinking." Josh was sitting on a chair against the wall. "Come here for a minute." He extended his arm to her. Hannah walked over to where he was sitting and sat down in his lap as he reached his hand around her. "Honey, you know there's a tour this weekend."

"Yeah, I know. It was sure nice of Mr. Whitney to excuse you so you can stay home to be with Sarah."

"Yes, it was, but I've been sitting here thinking about that. I think I should go."

"Why? Mr. Whitney said— "

"I know what he said," Josh interrupted. "But I think it's important that I go."

"Don't you think it's important to stay home when your daughter is in the hospital? How can you leave, knowing that she may not even live?"

"I can't afford to miss the tour because we'll need the money to pay for medical expenses. She'll be in the hospital for at least two or three months. With our deductible and the out of pocket costs, we'll owe thousands of dollars before our insurance kicks in."

Hannah sighed as she leaned against him. "I know, but

can't you stay home just this once? Please, Josh? I need you here, and so does Sarah."

"Oh, babe. I hate leaving you home alone. But I have to go… for us. I want us to be ahead. Don't you understand?"

"Yeah, I guess I do," Hannah said, not wanting to get into another argument. "We can talk more about this tomorrow. Let's go back to bed." She stood up, but he stayed seated, looking at the floor. Sadly, she went back to their bedroom, hoping he'd join her soon.

She lay there by herself, thinking about the decision that Josh had made. It just didn't seem right for him to leave her during a crisis like this. Sure, he had claimed to be doing it to get ahead of their mounting hospital bills. *But is that the real reason? Or is there more to it?* She simply could not understand why he seemed to think bills were more important than being with her.

HANNAH WAS in the kitchen fixing breakfast when Josh came downstairs on Friday morning. He sniffed hungrily as he entered the kitchen. "Morning, honey. Something sure smells good. Bacon and eggs? Yum."

"Morning. Breakfast is almost ready." She replied, trying to be polite. Truthfully, she was still frustrated about their discussion last night. It didn't help that she was starting to get yet another headache. She planned to take the new pills as soon as he left.

"I sure wish you were going with me this weekend."

"And I sure wish you were staying home this weekend," she replied, her back to him as she was facing the stove, fixing plates for the two of them.

Josh pulled out his chair and sat down at the table. "Honey, we've already been through this."

"Yeah, I know." Hannah turned to face him, with plates of food in her hands. "But I don't want you to go. I need you here... I... won't you please reconsider? She put their plates down on the table and sat down. "Just this once?"

"Hon, I'm really worried about the bills and-"

"Excuse me," she said as she abruptly got up and left the kitchen. Moments later, he heard the bedroom door slam shut. He followed her upstairs and into the bedroom. Hannah was sitting on the edge of the bed. He sat down beside her and started to put his arm around her.

"Honey, please––"

She pulled away from him. "No, Josh! I don't want to be alone if Sarah dies!"

Josh took her hand. Honey, I do understand. But I'm only going to be a couple of hours away. If anything, anything at all changes with Sarah, you can call the hotel, and I'll come back right away. I believe what Mrs. Whitney said. The Lord will be with us and watch out for our little girl."

Hannah, tired of what seemed to be constant fighting lately, sighed and said, "I'll probably be at the hospital most the time anyway, and I'm sure Mrs. Whitney and I will get together sometime over the weekend."

LATER THAT MORNING, Josh and Hannah walked into the airport. Josh checked in at the desk, then held Hannah's hand as they walked to the security gate where they would say their goodbyes. He embraced her in a hug, then kissed her tenderly.

Hannah forced a smile. "See you Sunday."

Flight 207 to Seattle is boarding at gate 10. Flight 207 is now boarding at gate 10 came the voice over the loudspeaker.

Josh took Hannah's hand in his own. "Well, I guess that's me. You'll be okay?"

"Yeah, I-I'll be fine," she said, not really believing it.

"Everything will be okay," he said, squeezing her hand.

Hannah looked at the gate. "Everyone else's boarding the plane. I guess you better go."

"I guess so," Josh said as he brushed a tear from her eye, then leaned over and kissed her tenderly on the lips.

She gave him a half-hearted return kiss, then put her arms around his neck and hugged him tightly. "Bye," was all she could manage. The pills did help, but at least it was only a dull throb now, not searing pain like before.

"I love you, darling. I'll call you when we get there, and again tonight, after the show." Josh released her, then turned and walked through the security gate. Feeling more dejected than ever, Hannah turned and made her way through the crowded airport out to the parking lot.

She glanced at her watch as she drove out of the airport parking lot. 8:45 a.m. It would be close to 9:30 a.m. when she would arrive at the hospital. She wondered how Sarah was doing. *Will there be any improvement in her condition today?*

Hannah sighed. *Why can't he understand how I feel?* She thought about her baby so close to death. She had suddenly felt nauseous and a little dizzy. She pulled over to the side of the road for a moment to clear her head.

4 - SARAH'S SONG

*J*osh opened his backpack to look for the book he had brought along for the trip. When he pulled it out, an envelope fell to the floor. He opened it and removed the card, reading it silently.

Lance was sitting in the seat next to Josh. Looking at him, he said, "Is something bothering you? You seem kind of distant this morning."

Josh was thinking back on the distance he had felt from Hannah as they had said their goodbyes at the airport. "I shouldn't be here, Mr. Whitney."

"What do you mean?"

"Read this." Josh handed him the card and waited while he read it.

"It's a very nice card, Josh. But I don't quite understand what you're trying to say."

Josh poured out his thoughts. "The card says, *To my wonderful husband.*' If I'm so wonderful, why did I feel so strongly I had to go on this tour? Hannah begged me to stay home. She's never done that before. She said that she doesn't want to be home alone with Sarah... saying she's worried that Sarah will die while I'm gone. Maybe I shouldn't have left." He couldn't remember ever feeling this guilty about something he had done.

"Josh, why exactly did you decide you had to come?"

"Well, we will need the money to pay for Sarah's hospital bills. They'll be thousands of dollars."

"Is that the only reason?"

"Well, yeah." More guilt, as he looked down. He felt flushed.

Lance shook his head. "I don't buy that, Josh. I've never known you to leave Hannah alone during a crisis. Tell me the truth."

Josh continued to look down at his feet, searching for words that weren't ready to come out yet.

"I offered to excuse you from this tour because I thought you would want to be home with your family. I could've easily insisted that you stay home, but I felt that it needed to be your decision."

Josh, now feeling ashamed of himself, turned to face Mr. Whitney, before finally saying, "Sir, can I be honest with you?"

Lance nodded. "I wish you would."

"I didn't really want to come. I wanted to stay home with Hannah. She needs me at home, and I need her. But I felt the need to get away and think things over. Sarah will be in the hospital for months, she'll never be like other kids, she will always require special care and therapy."

"Josh, Hannah needs you now. You need to be strong for her."

Josh was silent for a moment as his eyes began to water. "What about me? Ever since Sarah was born, everyone has said that I need to be strong for Hannah, that she's having a hard time dealing with this. Sarah is my child too. Does everyone think this is any easier for me? My heart breaks every time I see our little baby. How can I help Hannah when I'm hurting just as bad as she is? Sometimes I feel like God has abandoned us."

Lance realized that Josh was right. He certainly hadn't taken into consideration that Josh might be hurting too. "I'm sorry, Josh. I guess I never thought about how you must be feeling about all of this."

"I thought that maybe if I came on this tour, I would be able to sort out my own thoughts and feelings so that when I get home, I would be able to be stronger for Hannah. But I was wrong. The pain is worse when I'm not at home with her when she needs me the most."

"Then I suggest as soon as we land, you take the first available flight back home." He put his hand on his shoulder, and continued, "And God has not abandoned you. That I'm sure of. I will pray for you, Hannah and Sarah."

AFTER THEY HAD LANDED, Josh booked a return flight home and called Hannah to let her know. During his flight back, he spent the time contemplating what Mr. Whitney had said and tried to pray, even begging God to be with them. But he still felt empty.

Back home, he quietly slipped in the bed beside Hannah. It was late Friday night, and he didn't want to wake her. He reached over and lightly rubbed her cheek, then leaned over and kissed her. "I love you, babe," he whispered softly as he kissed her again. He snuggled close to her, wishing she was awake so we could tell her how much he loved her and their baby. After a while, he drifted off to sleep but was awakened a short time later by sobs. He leaned over and turned on the bedside lamp. "Hon, what's wrong?"

She reached for a Kleenex on the nightstand and wiped her eyes, then replied, "I'm so glad you're home. I'm so afraid we're going to lose our baby. Dr. Hampton doesn't give us much hope. He said that she may need a miracle to pull through."

Josh drew her into his arms and held her close to him, gently caressing her hair. "I'm so sorry, darling. I never should've left you to face this alone. I promise I won't go on another tour without discussing it with you first, and not until Sarah comes home from the hospital.

Hannah hugged him tightly. "I love you so much, Josh. I just felt so alone without you here. Mrs. Whitney spent some time with me at the hospital, but it just wasn't the same as having you there."

"She was there for you when I should've been. Will you forgive me?"

"Of course. You were only doing what you thought you had to do."

"Yeah, I guess I was. But hon... I..." Josh wrestled with his guilt about the real reason he left her to go on the tour. But she looked tired. *I'll tell her later.* "I'm glad I'm home."

Hannah yawned. "I'm glad too," she said softly as she drifted off to sleep.

5 - SARAH'S SONG

*H*annah awoke early on Thanksgiving morning, a few weeks later. She got up quietly, not wanting to wake Josh. She came out of the shower as Josh was just waking up.

"What time is it?" He asked.

"Eight-thirty."

He yawned as he stretched his arms out. "Why did you let me sleep so late?"

"Because today is Thanksgiving, and I thought you'd like to sleep in."

"Oh. What time are we supposed to be at Scott and Karen's?"

"One o'clock. Can we stop at the hospital to see Sarah before we go to the party?"

"Of course, we can."

Hannah was silent for a few moments, then she asked, "Do you think she'll ever be well enough to come home?"

"I don't know. The doctors are doing everything they can for her."

"I know," Hannah said softly. "But it hurts to think that she may never come home. We've never even held her or touched her."

Josh kissed her. "We'll get to bring her home. You'll see."

"But what if-?" Hannah couldn't continue. She buried her face in his chest and cried. Josh held her and let her cry. He knew how very deeply it hurt her to see little Sarah and knowing that her chances of surviving were very slim. After a few minutes, Hannah stopped crying. "Tomorrow was her due date. If only I— "

"Shush! Don't start that again. We both know that Sarah's premature birth was not your fault. You did everything the doctor told you to do."

"You think maybe she'll be home by Christmas?"

"I hope so."

"I do, too," she said as she squeezed his hand. "I'll fix breakfast while you take your shower."

While she was making the coffee, the phone rang. "Hello? Hi, Dr. Hampton. Yes, we plan on stopping by at noon. Has there been any change? Yeah, sure. Okay. We'll see you then."

"Who was on the phone?" Josh said as he entered the kitchen.

"That was Dr. Hampton. He said there's a specialist there that has been in spending some time working with Sarah. She would like to talk to us."

"Did he say what about?"

Hannah shook her head. "No, but it didn't sound good. There hasn't been any change in her."

AT NOON, Josh and Hannah walked hand in hand to the NICU.

Dr. Hampton was standing at the nurse's station and greeted them each with a handshake. "Please come into my office." They followed him down the hall and into his office.

"Mr. and Mrs. Bryton, I'd like you to meet Dr. Julie Ridgemont. She specializes in premature infants."

Dr. Ridgemont smiled at the young couple. "Nice to meet you both," she said as she shook their hands. "Please have a seat." Josh and Hannah sat down as Dr. Ridgemont sat down at the desk and opened the folder in front of her. She was silent for a moment as she read over her notes, then folded her hands on the desk.

"I've reviewed your daughter's file, and I have examined her. Dr. Hampton informed me he has already explained some of the complications of being born two months early, such as the RDS, why she needs the ventilator and her digestive issues. I concur with Dr. Hampton's treatment so far." She paused while looking down at her notes.

"How long will she have to stay in the NICU?" Hannah asked.

"There's no way of knowing." Dr. Ridgemont answered. "Every child is different. It could be weeks. Could be months. We don't know. I wish I had a better answer for you."

Josh and Hannah were silent for a moment. "Is… is our daughter going to die?" Josh asked, his voice barely above a whisper."

Dr. Ridgemont took a deep breath. "I wish I could tell you

that Sarah will be ok, that she will start breathing on her own, but I can't. We have no way of knowing. But I can tell you this. Don't give up on her. There are babies that have been in her condition that have recovered completely with no breathing issues at all and have grown into happy, healthy children. "

"You said you think she has other issues. Like what?" Josh asked.

"We need to do more tests, but we suspect Spina Bifida. However, we are more concerned with her breathing right now." Dr. Ridgemont answered. "We will address the other issues after we get her through this."

Hannah took a deep breath. "In other words, you're saying that if Sarah dies, there won't be any need to talk about her other issues."

Dr. Ridgemont shook her head. "I'm not saying that at all, Mrs. Bryton. I'm just saying that we need to get her breathing on her own. That's our top priority right now. Everything else needs to take a back seat. She is a fighter, and we need to help her fight. But, having said all that, there's one other possibility that may be necessary. If she starts breathing on her own, it's likely she may need to be placed in an institution that specializes in this kind of care."

Josh and Hannah both sat there silently, trying to imagine how these new developments would affect Sarah and themselves.

Without saying anything more about what they had just been informed about, Josh thanked them and turned to leave with Hannah. Hannah looked like she was in shock after the comment about Spina Bifida. But she paused at the door and turned around to face the two Doctors. "Thank you both. I…" She started sobbing and was unable to continue.

Josh put his arm around her, and they left the room, Hannah still sobbing.

THAT AFTERNOON, Josh and Hannah arrived at the home of the Whitney's son Scott. Josh rang the doorbell, and seconds later, the door was opened by Karen, Scott's wife, who greeted them each with a hug. "Come on in. Happy Thanksgiving. Josh and Hannah followed Karen past the kitchen and into the living room. Lance and Emilie Whitney were seated on the couch with her two grandsons, Scotty and Kevin.

Karen excused herself to go help her husband Scott in the kitchen.

"How is Sarah doing? Lance asked.

"No change," Josh answered.

Lance nodded his understanding.

The doorbell rang. A minute later, Karen came into the room, followed by another young couple and their four children.

"Josh and Hannah, I'd like you to meet my sister Dyane and her husband, Mark. And these are their children, Matthew, Jordan, Nicole, and little Courtney. Mark and Dyane, I like you to meet Josh and Hannah Bryton."

A few moments later, Scott announced that dinner was ready. As Josh and Hannah were following others into the dining room, Josh leaned over and whispered, "I know you're upset about what Dr. Ridgemont said, but please try to be cheerful."

"I'll do the best I can," Hannah whispered back as she forced herself to smile. She knew that Josh was right. She didn't want to spoil the other's Thanksgiving.

Josh and Hannah were seated across the table from Mark and Dyane, and Dyane held baby Courtney. Hannah wondered, *will I ever hold my own baby like that.*

After the meal was over, everyone gathered in the living room. The older children were sitting on the floor, doing puzzles and coloring, and Karen was holding Courtney.

"She sure is a good little baby, Dy. What's your secret for keeping her so quiet all the time?" Karen asked her sister.

"No secret. She's very easy to please. Nicole was that way too, but Matt and Jordan were just the opposite."

Karen laughed. "I remember. They were very impatient little boys. Come to think of it, so was Scotty. Kevin is a bit quieter."

Before long, everyone was talking about their children. Remembering things that the children had done or said. Even Lance and Emilie were talking about things that their three children had done when they were small.

Hannah glanced over at Josh. Even he was laughing along with the others. *How can he be so happy?* She wondered. He had a child too, but he couldn't share any stories. They didn't have any 'normal' stories to tell about their only child.

"Courtney still likes to get up in the middle of the night," Dyane said. "I keep hoping that one of these days she'll realize that nighttime is for sleeping." Everyone laughed.

"I know what you mean," Karen agreed. "But it is wonderful to have children. Sometimes I wonder what I ever did before I had the boys."

"Me too. I don't know what I would do if anything ever happened to one of our kids." Dyane said.

Hannah's eyes teared up, and suddenly she could take it no longer. She quickly got up and ran outside. The others stared after her, not understanding.

Josh excused himself and went after her.

Is she okay?" Dyane asked, worried.

"It must have something to do with Sarah," Emilie said. Then she explained Sarah's condition to them.

JOSH FOUND Hannah leaning against a large oak tree. He put his hand on her shoulder. "Are you okay, honey?"

"I'm—I'm sorry. But I just couldn't stay there any longer. It hurts, Josh."

"I know," Josh whispered. "I feel the pain too."

"But you were laughing with the rest of them. They all have stories to tell about their children—stories we may never have."

"I may have been laughing on the outside, but I was crying on the inside. I was only putting up a front for the sake of the other guests."

"If only I could be that strong," Hannah said softly.

"Honey, please come back inside."

"You go ahead. I'd like to be alone for a few minutes."

Okay, but don't stay long. It's kind of chilly."

"I won't. I just need a few minutes to myself."

Josh kissed her, then went back inside.

SCOTT LOOKED up as he came in. "Everything okay?

Josh nodded. "She'll be fine. She said to tell everyone she's sorry."

"We're sorry, Josh," Karen said. "Emilie explained how Sarah is still in the hospital and on a respirator. When we were talking about our kids...I can't imagine how you and Hannah must've been feeling. Seeing her on a respirator, and not being able to hold her."

Josh shook his head. "Thank you." He paused for a moment and continued. "But there is something else we found out."

"What's that? Lance asked.

"Before we came here today, we stopped at the hospital. We met with Dr. Ridgemont, a specialist for babies like Sarah. She talked to us about some of the potential problems and difficulties that we may be facing when she gets older because of the RDS. We had already considered some of that. But then she said she suspects Sarah may have Spina Bifida but doesn't want to talk about that until they get her breathing under control. Hannah...well, we both had a hard time with that, with everything else going on."

The others stared at them and were silent as they digested the awful news.

Hannah came back in, and Karen went over to her.

She took Hannah's hand into her own. "I'm so sorry you are going through this. If there is anything we can do, please let us know."

"Thank you," Hannah replied, barely above a whisper. Karen released her hand. "We'll pray for her."

6 - SARAH'S SONG

*H*annah remained awake long after Josh had gone to sleep that night. She had tossed and turned for several hours but still could not go to sleep. She looked over at Josh. He was sleeping so soundly. She got up, and not bothering to put a robe on, quietly walked down the hall. She paused for a moment, her hand at the doorknob of Sarah's bedroom door.

After going in, she stared into the darkness for a few moments before turning on the light. She thought about how quiet and empty it was. The room was decorated with soft pastel colors. Hannah lightly touched her crib that had come from Mississippi, a gift from Josh's parents and two sisters. The crib stood against one wall, with the changing table and dresser against another wall. Diapers were stacked neatly, untouched. The beautiful oak rocking chair, a gift from Josh, sat in one corner of the room. Hannah jumped slightly when she felt a gentle touch on the shoulder. She turned to see Josh standing beside her. "Are you okay?"

"Yeah, I was just thinking, that's all."

Josh took her hand in his and led her over to the rocking chair. He sat down, pulling her onto his lap. "You haven't slept at all, have you?"

"I couldn't. I'm sorry I woke you."

"I guess it wasn't a very happy Thanksgiving, was it?"

"When everyone else started talking about their kids and how thankful they are for them and telling stories, I...I wondered if we would ever have stories to share about Sarah. I wanted to get out of there, to run away. They kept saying how thankful they are, while I was asking myself what I had to be thankful for. Our baby is in the hospital, fighting for her life."

Hannah paused for a moment as she rested her head on Josh's shoulder. Now, crying as she continued, "I've never been able to hold her or feed her. We've only seen her through a window. I didn't feel thankful. I felt angry. Angry because our baby has to suffer so much just to stay alive. I felt angry because I kept thinking that I'm responsible for the way she is. I thought that if I hadn't spent that day out of bed...maybe I wouldn't have gone into labor so early. And, I even felt angry at God for allowing her to be born like that."

Hannah paused again, giving Josh a chance to speak.

"Oh, darling. None of this is your fault. You've got to believe that. There is nothing you could do to prevent going into labor that night."

"Maybe...I guess..." Hannah yawned. "What time is it?"

"Two forty-five," Josh answered. "We should go back to bed."

Hannah wrapped her arms around his neck, her head still

resting on his shoulder. He picked her up and carried her back to their bedroom.

~~~~~~

AS THE NEXT several weeks passed, Josh and Hannah spent very little time at home. Most of the time, they were either at work or at the hospital. Hannah had decided to return to work shortly after Thanksgiving, and they both were excused from overnight road trips until Sarah could be released from the hospital.

There had been very little change in little Sarah's condition, and the Dr.'s didn't think she would make it to Christmas, but the tiny infant continued to fight. They continued to pray constantly for her life.

Hannah woke early on the morning of December 20th. The alarm would go off soon, and she needed a few minutes to herself before Josh got up. She wanted to talk to him but wasn't quite sure how. It was only five days until Christmas, and there was only one thing that she wanted. She hoped that he would agree.

When Josh woke up a short time later, Hannah was sitting in the chair, staring out the window. Her mind seemed to be a million miles away.

"A penny for your thoughts?" He asked.

"Josh, I've been thinking. Christmas is in five days. You know what I want more than anything?"

"What's that?" He asked.

She took a deep breath, and staring straight into his eyes, said, "I want to bring Sarah home. I want to touch her and hold her. I want to have our baby here with us." Almost crying now, she continued, "I know she may not live much longer, but I want to have her with us, not in the hospital. Please, Josh? Can we bring Sarah home?"

Josh got up and walked over and embraced her. "Darling, I want Sarah to come home too. Let's talk to Dr. Hampton today about having her home for Christmas."

"Thank you!" Now, relieved, she hugged him back tightly.

"I want her home just as much as you do. In fact, let's go to the hospital now. I'll call Mr. Whitney and tell him that we need to talk to Dr. Hampton. He'll understand, and I'm sure he'll understand us being late.

"Yeah, lets. Oh, Josh. I hope they'll let us bring her home. I want our little girl to experience all the love we can give her."

"Yes, we do have a lot of love to give her."

Hannah kissed him on the cheek, then went into the bathroom to shower.

I hope they let us bring her home, Josh thought to himself.

"I THINK you would be making a big mistake," Dr. Hampton said when they told him that they wanted to take Sarah home. "Your baby is very fragile. She requires very special care. It can take more than an hour to feed her."

"I can give her all the time she needs," Hannah argued.

"She also requires extensive medical attention. She'll probably never learn to walk or talk or do what other children do. I've already told you that she may not make it until

Christmas. She is still very weak. Her lungs have shown some improvement, but I don't know if it's enough for her to breathe without the ventilator."

"Dr. Hampton, my wife, and I love Sarah, and we are willing to take that chance. Maybe she won't live past the first day at home, but at least we will be able to spend a little time with her, caring for her, and giving her all the love we can. We want to experience the joy of being parents. Please let us take our baby home."

"Don't you think we're capable of caring for her?" Hannah asked.

"I'm sure you will do your best to care for her. I have seen your love for her during the past few months."

"Our love for her started before she was even born," Hannah said. "We're never gonna stop loving her. She was conceived because Josh and I love each other and wanted to share that love with a child. Maybe Sarah won't be like other children, but she is ours. And we won't love her less just because of the way she is."

Dr. Hampton looked silently at them. "Alright. Since she has shown some improvement, we can try to take her off the respirator. If she can breathe on her own, then it may be possible to release her. However, if we need to put her back on the respirator, then it won't be possible to let her go."

"Are you saying that if she can breathe on her own, we can take her home?" Josh asked.

Yes. If she breaths on her own, she will be watched around the clock. If she does okay for a few days, then maybe I can release her. Possibly even by Christmas Day. But if we need to put her back on the respirator, I'm afraid I won't be able to release her. Is that fair enough?"

Hannah looked at Josh, then at Dr. Hampton. "We'll accept that," Hannah said. "And she will make it. We will have our baby home for Christmas."

"There's one more thing before you make your final decision. I would like you to talk to Dr. Ridgemont again. She can better prepare you for what to expect from Sarah."

"As long as she doesn't tell us to put her in an institution. We won't do it," Hannah said.

"Very well then, let's go and see how she does."

Josh and Hannah followed him to the NICU. As they watched their baby through the window, they both prayed that she would start breathing on her own.

7 - SARAH'S SONG

*C*hristmas eve arrived. Josh and Hannah spent it at the home of Lance and Emilie Whitney, along with Scott, Karen, and their children. They were also joined by the Whitney's two other children, Samantha and her family, and Seth and his family.

After dinner that evening, everyone gathered in the living room to sing Christmas carols around the piano. It was almost 7:30 p.m. The phone rang, and Emilie went to answer it. A few minutes later, she returned. "Hannah, you're wanted on the phone. It's Dr. Hampton."

Karen stopped playing the piano, realizing that the phone call could bring bad news about Sarah. Hannah reached for her husband's hand, and together they went into the kitchen. Trembling, she picked up the receiver. "Hello?"

"Hello, Mrs. Bryton. It looks like your baby will be home for Christmas, after all. She's been off the respirator for four days, and she's doing well. We'll have her ready by ten o'clock tomorrow morning. Is that a convenient time for you?"

"We'll be there. Thank you, Dr. Hampton." Hannah hung up the phone and turned to face Josh. "Our baby is coming home. Tomorrow!"

"That's great!" Josh put his arm around her and went back into the living room. Both Josh and Hannah had tears of joy on their cheeks.

Lance was the first to speak. "What's wrong? Is it Sarah? Is she okay?"

"It was Dr. Hampton. We're bringing our baby home tomorrow."

"That's wonderful news!" Lance said. "Absolutely wonderful."

"How is she doing?" Karen asked.

Josh replied, "She's been taken off the respirator and is doing much better. We got the Christmas miracle we have been hoping and praying for!"

THE NEXT MORNING, Josh and Hannah arrived at the hospital, filled with anticipation about finally bringing their daughter home.

Hannah paused just inside the door and turned to face her husband. "Josh, what if we can't do this? Our baby is so tiny and fragile. What if—what if something happens?" Josh put his arm around her. He could readily understand her fears, for he felt the same and had the same questions in his own mind.

"Honey, everything will be okay. If Dr. Hampton didn't think so, he wouldn't let her go. We've been waiting for this day for three months. We will love her and care for her the best we know how."

Hannah nodded. "I hope you're right. I so much want to be a good mother."

"You'll be a wonderful mother. Now let's go get our daughter." They stepped into the elevator and eagerly awaited their arrival on the 4th floor.

They found Dr. Hampton waiting for them at the nurse's station. "Good morning, Mr. and Mrs. Bryton." He greeted them with a smile. "Your daughter is ready and waiting. How are you two feeling?"

"Excited. Nervous." Hannah answered.

"That's perfectly normal," Dr. Hampton reassured her. They followed him into the NICU. There they found their tiny daughter being held lovingly by Nurse Breezy, a grandmotherly type whom they had come to know well during the past few months. She smiled.

"She is all ready for her trip home." Connie tenderly placed the sleeping infant into her mother's waiting arms.

"Oh, Josh. Look at her. She is beautiful. No tubes or anything." Josh smiled as he gently touched his daughter's cheek. He placed the car seat in the nearby chair, and Hannah gently placed Sarah into it and strapped her in.

"Sarah has been doing well," Dr. Hampton said, "But don't hesitate to call if you have any questions or concerns. There will always be someone here to help. She does have special needs, but most of all, she needs what all children need--

love." With that, he handed them a few pages of instructions about the special care she would need.

"Thank you for all you've done for our baby. And for us." Josh said, shaking Dr. Hampton's hand. With that, the family of three left the NICU, hopefully for the last time.

HANNAH TURNED out the bedside lamp and slipped into bed beside Josh.

Josh put his arm around her and said, "It's been such a nice vacation. I almost wish we didn't have to go back to work tomorrow."

"Josh, I've been thinking. Maybe it's not such a good idea that I go back to work. I think it would be best if I quit the show."

"Quit the show? Honey, you've got to be kidding! You can't quit. We're a team. Our fans expect us to be together, and so does Mr. Whitney." Josh paused to catch his breath. "How long have you been thinking about this?"

"If you will calm down for a minute." Hannah paused for a moment, then continued. "I just don't feel that I should go back to work right now. I should stay at home with Sarah."

"Hannah, we've been on the show for over three years. It's more than a job. It's a career. You love it as much as I do. If you quit now, you'll regret it later." He thought about how hard they had practiced their act to prepare for the audition to get on the show. "Remember all the sacrifices we made, spending all the time practicing to get good enough to become professionals?"

Hannah thought about it, and inwardly agreed it had been a lot of work and time. *But Sarah has to come first.* "I have been thinking about it—ever since we brought her home from the hospital. I don't think I can take proper care of her and work at the same time. She needs special care, and we have such a hectic work schedule. I just don't think I can handle it."

"We'll do it together. Promise me you won't quit." Josh kissed her.

Hannah was silent for a moment. She wanted so much to do what she thought was best for their baby, but she also wanted to please her husband. She loved him and would do anything for him, even if it made her unhappy.

"Please, babe, promise me you won't quit," he begged.

"Okay, I promise," Hannah reluctantly agreed, then added, "But can't we at least talk about it?"

"What's to talk about?" Josh asked. "Mr. Whitney gave us permission to take her to work with us, and on the road trips as well. It will be okay. We'll take care of her together. We— "

He was interrupted by crying, coming from Sarah's bedroom. Hannah sighed as she got up. "I'll get her."

As Hannah rocked the baby, she knew that it would be a long night. Sarah had been home from the hospital for a week, and she seemed to have a sleeping schedule of her own —she would sleep during the day and stay awake most of the night. Hannah had lost a great deal of sleep during the past week, and she did not feel like going back to work in the morning. If only she could make Josh understand how she felt. Hannah kissed her daughter on the forehead. "Sarah, I'm so glad you're home. Your daddy and I missed you so much."

At 7:45 a.m. the next morning, Hannah carried Sarah into the girl's dressing room at the Lance Whitney studio. She was greeted by Amber, Kristi, and Kelly, all fellow performers.

"Hi, Hannah. And this must be the little princess we've heard so much about," Amber said as she got up to admire the tiny infant. "She sure is a beautiful baby. Mind if I hold her?"

"Sure," Hannah replied as she gently placed Sarah in Amber's arms, then sat down in the nearest chair.

"How was your Christmas vacation, Hannah?"

"It was nice, especially since Sarah came home."

"How is she doing? I mean, does she still have problems digesting her food?" Kristi asked.

"Well, she still has a lot of problems because she can't suck properly, and it usually takes almost an hour each feeding. And she has a very irregular sleeping pattern—she likes to stay up all night and sleep during the day."

"How are you doing?" Kelly asked, noticing how tired she looked. "You look like you could go back to bed."

"I've been more tired than usual because sometimes she'll get up about the time we go to bed and won't go back to sleep until really late. And she wakes up early. Josh sleeps through it all. Maybe once I get her into a regular sleeping schedule, I won't be so tired all the time. But I guess I better get used to it." Hannah sighed as she leaned back in her chair.

"What do you mean?" Kelly asked.

"Sarah has a lot of medical problems and will always require a great deal of special care. I don't know if I can work and take care of her. But Josh promised we'll handle it together."

8 - SARAH'S SONG

"*J*osh? Josh Bryton? Is it really you?"

Josh glanced up from his lunch. Seeing who it was, he set his sandwich onto the plate and stood up, shaking the man's hand. "Jeremy Reynolds! How are you doing? Boy, it has been a long time. Would you like to join us?" Josh asked, introducing him to Kevin, Peter, and Tyler, his friends from the show.

"Thanks, but I'm just on the way out to an appointment," Jeremy said. "So, what are you doing around here?"

"My wife and I are singers on the Lance Whitney show."

"Wow! I didn't even know you were married!" Jeremy looked at his watch as an alarm pinged. "Darn it, I have to run, but you know what? Rachel and I are having a few friends over for supper tonight. Why don't you and your wife come? We'd love to have you. Around six-thirty?"

"We'd love to if we can find a babysitter for our three-month-old daughter," Josh answered.

Jeremy wrote his address and phone number on a napkin

and handed it to Josh. "Give me a call and let me know. I really hope you can make it."

BACK AT THE STUDIO, Josh knocked on the door to the women's dressing room.

Kristi opened the door. "Hi, Josh. Come on in."

Josh entered the room and found Hannah sitting on the couch, giving Sarah her bottle. "Hey babe, I ran into an old friend of mine from San Lupo. He invited us over to his place for supper tonight. He and his wife are having a few friends over."

"What did you tell him?"

"That we'll be there if we can find a babysitter."

"Josh, I really don't feel like going out tonight. I'd just like to stay at home. I'm really tired. Can we make it another time?"

"Just for a little while?"

"I'm not ready to leave Sarah with the sitter. You go ahead and go."

"Aww, c'mon babe. It'll be fun. I used to love hanging out with Jeremy. He was one of my best friends."

Sighing, Hannah set the finished bottle down, once again feeling like she needed to please her husband. Grudgingly, she relented. "Alright. But please, let's not stay too late."

"Of course." Josh was eagerly anticipating spending time with Jeremy again.

"I'm glad we decided to come tonight, Honey." Josh said as they pulled up in front of Jeremy's house later that evening, "and it's good we brought Sarah. It's too soon for a sitter."

Hannah followed her husband to the door carrying a sleeping Sarah, but still not sure she had made the right decision. She was tired and would much rather be home.

Josh rang the doorbell, and they were greeted by Jeremy, who ushered them in and introduced them to his wife Rachel and several other friends who had gathered.

Hannah's mood lightened a little, as the other guests gushed over her daughter, each of the women eagerly taking their turn to hold the tiny child.

"Josh, it's getting late. We've got to work tomorrow," Hannah said as she glanced at the clock on the wall above the fireplace. It was almost midnight, and the other guests had all left.

"Hannah, I'm so glad you could come. I'm glad you brought little Sarah. She's a beautiful baby." Rachel Reynolds said with a smile.

"Thanks, we had a great time. But, Hannah's right. We better get home."

"Okay, let's do it again real soon. Maybe we can all get together for a tennis game or something." Jeremy suggested.

"That be great. Rachel, it's been nice meeting you. Thank you for the wonderful supper." Josh said. He put his arm around Hannah as they walked out and got into the car. "It was a great evening, wasn't it? Aren't you glad you decided to come?" Josh asked as he pulled the car onto the highway.

Hannah leaned back and closed her eyes, not bothering to answer him.

"Hannah, are you upset?" Josh asked.

"You know I didn't want to go tonight. Why did we have to stay so late? Everyone else left at 10 p.m., and you promised we wouldn't stay late."

"I know, but Jeremy and I were best friends. After college, we both went our separate ways. We had a lot to talk about. I thought you would be more understanding."

"Josh, I do understand. Jeremy and Rachel are very nice, but you don't even try to understand how I feel. You wouldn't listen to me last night, and you didn't listen to me today."

"If you're talking about quitting again—"

Hannah interrupted, "Oh, forget it, Josh! Let's just drop it." They rode the rest of the way home in silence.

"Sorry," he mumbled. Not wanting to anger her further, he stayed silent the rest of the way home.

9 - SARAH'S SONG

*T*hree weeks later, Hannah carried Sarah into the clinic for her first monthly check-up.

The nurse smiled. "Good afternoon, Mrs. Bryton. You can go in. Dr. Hampton will be right with you."

"Thank you," Hannah said as she went into his office.

A few minutes later, Dr. Hampton came in. "Hi, Mrs. Bryton. How are you today?"

"Okay, I guess."

"And how is little Sarah?"

"She seems to be doing ok in most respects, but feeding is often a challenge because she tends to spit the food back out a lot."

Dr. Hampton carefully placed the child on the scale. "Not quite five and a half, a small gain since she left the NICU. That's a good sign." He examined her ears, eyes, heart, and reflexes, and gave her back to Hannah.

Then he looked closely at Hannah. She looked tired. "Tell me how you're doing, Mrs. Bryton."

"I go to the studio every day from eight to five. Sarah goes to bed at eight, but most nights, she wakes up again shortly after we go to bed. She doesn't always go back to sleep for several hours. I guess I'm having trouble handling a new baby and our hectic work schedule."

"I see." He made some notes. "Have you considered quitting your job? A baby like Sarah can be a full-time job in itself."

Hannah nodded. "Yeah, but my husband won't even talk about it. He doesn't think I should."

"I think maybe you should at least take a leave of absence for a while."

"I wouldn't mind that at all, but Josh won't go for that either," Hannah said.

"You said you have trouble sleeping at night?"

Hannah nodded. "No matter what time I go to bed, it seems like I can't get to sleep because I know that Sarah is going to wake up. "

"I can give you a prescription for a sleeping pill."

Hannah shook her head. "I don't want sleeping pills. I'm afraid I won't hear Sarah when she wakes up.

"Well, you could try Melatonin then. It's non-prescription, but it might help." He made some more notes. "Anything else?"

"I've also gotten some extremely bad headaches. They're agonizing, and sometimes make me nauseous, and dizzy." She placed her hand at the side of her head. "In fact, I had one coming on before I got here, but the aspirin doesn't seem to help."

"I would say that qualifies as migraines. They're often

caused by stress. From everything you've told me, I think you're trying to do too much. Between your job and Sarah, and not sleeping at night, you need to start taking it easy. Talk to your husband. Tell him how you have been feeling. I'm sure you will agree that you need some time off." He logged into his computer. "I'll give you a prescription for the migraines that will be stronger than aspirin."

"Josh doesn't like pills, but I need to do something. I can't take care of Sarah if I can barely stand up." She thanked him, then left the clinic, wondering if Josh would understand.

She stopped at the pharmacy on the way home, filled the prescription for the migraines, and bought some Melatonin. She nodded absently as the pharmacist explained the dosage and warned of the possible side effects, but she really wasn't paying attention, as she was worried about what she would tell Josh about them. She thought about his aunt that had gotten addicted to opioids and died of an overdose. He had taken her death hard and had avoided any kind of prescription pills since then and expected her to do the same. He even went as far as following anti-vaccination groups on the internet. She had a little more faith in medicine then he did but understood. That would be hard on anybody. She thought to herself, *At least I won't have to take them for long as Sarah seems to be getting better,* justifying her decision not to tell Josh.

HANNAH OPENED HER EYES. The soft light of the clock showed 3:05 AM. As her eyes begin to close again, she could hear the baby crying. Quietly, she got up and went into her four-month-old daughter's bedroom. She was relieved that Dr. Hampton had considered her concerns about sleeping pills, and instead suggested she take Melatonin. It had made it easier to fall asleep, but she could still hear Sarah when she woke up crying at night.

She picked her child up, speaking softly. "It's okay, Princess." After Sarah had been changed, Hannah took her down to the kitchen to fix her a bottle.

She sat down in the rocking chair in the living room and begin feeding her. As she looked down into the tiny face and hands, an overwhelming feeling of love came over her. Hannah lightly kissed Sarah's cheek. "I love you, Sarah Joylynn Bryton."

HANNAH AND SARAH were alone in the girl's dressing room at the studio the next afternoon. Everyone else had gone to lunch, including Josh. She had chosen to skip her lunch, hoping to get a little rest. Sarah would often sleep during the day, and even a short nap would be a godsend to Hannah. As she was about to doze off, a light knock on the door surprised her. She had thought that everyone was gone. "Come in." The door opened, and Lance came in.

"Can we talk for a few minutes, Hannah?"

"Sure, Mr. Whitney. Is something wrong?"

"That's what I'd like to know. I've been watching you, Hannah. Is everything okay at home? Are you and Josh having problems?"

"No, sir," Hannah replied. "Why do you ask?"

"These past few weeks, I've noticed that you've been tired, and sometimes irritable, especially with Josh. I've never known you to be so short-tempered with him before. Whatever is bothering you, it's also beginning to show in your job performance. Do you have anything that you would like to say?"

Hannah looked down at Sarah, then back up at Mr. Whitney. She took a breath and said, "Yes, sir. I would like to be excused from the upcoming tour."

Surprised, Lance replied, "May I ask why?"

"I feel it's necessary for me to stay at home with Sarah. She has so many special needs."

Lance looked down at the sleeping infant. "Sarah is a very special child, and I know how much she means to you and Josh, but our fans expect all of us to be there. We've already agreed that you may take Sarah on the tours."

"Please, Mr. Whitney. Just this once. I've been so tired lately since Sarah came home from the hospital. I need some time off."

Lance, again looked at Sarah, still sleeping peacefully. "I was going to tell everyone after lunch, but I guess you should know now. The T.V. network called, and they confirmed they would like to film a few shows to evaluate us for an upcoming slot to host the Gospel Hour. And you know how much that means to everyone, how hard we've all worked."

Lance noticed the tears in her eyes, and his tone softened. "Hannah, I know you want to be excused, but we already have Leo out with a broken leg, and Aimee out on personal leave after the passing of her mother. I can't lose anyone else right now. After we complete this tour, we will sit down and talk about you taking some family medical leave."

"I understand, Mr. Whitney. That's wonderful they're considering us for the show. Thank you for listening." She felt relieved, knowing that even though she still needed to go on this tour, she would get some time off soon. She just needed to be strong for a few more shows.

10 - SARAH'S SONG

*T*hat evening during supper, Hannah only picked at her food.

Josh cleared his throat.

"Honey, I invited Jeremy and Rachel over this evening. I know I should have asked first but––"

Hannah interrupted, "Are you serious, Josh? Why? You know I have been so tired lately. I'm just not up to having company."

"Hannah, they had us over, so I thought it would be nice to invite them here. I promise it won't be a late night."

Hannah grunted. "Ha. That's what you said the night we went over there. I don't want company, Josh!"

She abruptly got up and went upstairs. After putting on her pajamas, she sighed as she laid down on the bed. She felt so tired and worn out, yet no one seemed to care or understand, not even her husband.

After Hannah had gone upstairs, Josh finished his supper,

thinking about their argument. *Why did she get so angry? Lately, she's been so touchy. Everything seems to upset her.*

Josh picked up the phone and dialed Jeremy's number. "Hi, Jeremy. Would you be okay with you if we got together another time? It's been kind of a long day at work, and Hannah isn't feeling well."

"Sure, Josh. I hope she feels better."

Josh hung up the phone and went upstairs. Hannah was lying in bed with Sarah beside her. He looked at her for a moment, then said, "I called Jeremy and told him not to come. I don't think they should be here when we're fighting."

"Well, we wouldn't be fighting if you had talked to me first before asking them over." Hannah snapped.

"I guess I didn't realize that I had to ask permission to invite friends over." Josh snapped back. "Since you don't seem to want my friends here, maybe you don't want me here either."

Hannah watched in silence as he stormed out of the bedroom. Seconds later, she heard the front door slam shut. "Well, Sarah, I don't blame your daddy for leaving. But don't you worry, little one, I will never leave you." Hannah gently touched Sarah's cheek with her index finger, singing softly as she did so. Within minutes, Sarah and Hannah were asleep.

HANNAH SIGHED as she sat down on the porch. It was almost eight o'clock when Josh pulled into the driveway. He paused and looked down at her before going into the house, but neither of them spoke. Hannah started to cry. She was so tired. If only Josh would try to understand how she felt. She buried her face in her hands and was unaware he had come back outside until she felt a light touch on her shoulder.

She looked up to see Josh standing beside her. For a moment, neither of them spoke, then Hannah said softly, barely above a whisper. "I-I'm sorry, Josh. I had no right to get so upset."

Josh sat down beside her and looked into her tear-filled eyes and noticed how tired she looked. The sparkle that was usually in her eyes was no longer there. It was replaced by sadness. "I should've talked to you first," Josh said.

"I'm sorry too. It's just that lately I've been so tired. Sarah gets up at all hours of the night. I never get much sleep. We're up early to get ready for work. I just haven't felt like myself."

"Honey, maybe it would be a good idea if we asked Mr. Whitney to excuse you from the tour. I know the T.V. show filming is important to everyone, but— "

"He won't excuse me. I've already talked to him. He needs us because, with Leo and Aimee out, he can't fill the program if we're gone too. But he did say, after this tour, I could take a leave of absence.

Josh put his arm around her. "Honey, it's me who owes you an apology. I haven't been helping much with Sarah since we brought her home from the hospital. Honestly, I wasn't sure if I have the patience to take an hour to feed her, But, from now on, I'll get up with her.'"

Hannah, grateful for even that small respite, replied, "Would you really? That would be great if I could get a good night's sleep for a change." She hugged him before they went in.

HANNAH SANK down on the bed in the motel room that she and Josh were sharing with Mr. and Mrs. Whitney. The flight from Los Angeles to Bellevue, Washington, hadn't been very pleasant for her, and she felt another migraine coming on.

Sarah had been fussy, and Hannah had felt nauseous during most of the trip. She had done her best to hide the way she was feeling from the others. She glanced up as Josh came out of the bathroom.

"Honey, I'm going downstairs to the coffee shop with the others. Want to come down?"

Hannah shook her head. "You go ahead. I'm kind of tired. I'd like to lie down and rest."

"Okay. I'll be back later."

Hannah nodded as he left the room. She looked at Sarah, now asleep in her arms. Gently, Hannah laid her in the porta-crib, then laid down on the bed herself. Within minutes she fell asleep. When Hannah awoke a short time later, Emilie was sitting on the other bed reading a book. "Hi, Mrs. Whitney. I thought you were with the others."

"I was, but I came back because I'm worried about you. Are you okay?"

"I'm fine," Hannah whispered. "Why do you ask?"

"You didn't look like you felt well on the plane, and you look so tired. Are you sure you're okay?" Emilie sat down on the bed beside Hannah and touched her flushed cheek. "You do feel a little warm. I'd better talk to Lance about excusing you from tonight's show."

"Please don't, Mrs. Whitney. I have to perform tonight. Everyone needs to be there for the T.V. show filming. I can't let them down."

"But you need to think about yourself too. You shouldn't be working when you're not feeling well."

"I'm sure it'll pass. Please don't say anything to Josh or Mr. Whitney."

Emilie gave her a hug. "Okay. I won't say anything for now, but you have to promise me you'll get some rest."

Hannah promised and was grateful when Mrs. Whitney left so she could lay back down.

JOSH WOKE up late that night, not sure what had awakened him. Then he realized it was Hannah moving restlessly beside him, moaning something that he couldn't understand. Must be a dream, he told himself. He rolled over to go back to sleep. A few minutes later, Hannah sat bolt upright in bed and screamed his name.

In an instant, the light came on, and the Whitney's woke up. Both were looking at her with alarm on their faces. As Josh held her, he could feel her body trembling. She was sweating and crying hysterically, barely able to catch her breath. Josh gently rubbed her cheek, speaking softly. "Everything is okay. I'm right here. Calm down. It was only a dream."

"P-promise me...you'll never leave me." Hannah managed to gasp.

"Of course, I'll never leave you. What were you dreaming about?"

Hannah clung tightly to him as though she would never let him go. "It was so awful. It was-- " Hannah paused, unable to continue.

"It's okay now," Josh said soothingly. "I'm right here." Josh held her until she drifted off to sleep.

Emily, keeping her voice down, asked, "I wonder what caused that. Does she often have nightmares?"

"No. She hasn't been herself lately," Josh answered. He looked down at Hannah, still sleeping. "I think a lot of it has to do with adjusting to having a new baby. Sarah kind of has a schedule of her own."

"How is Sarah been doing?" Lance asked, also keeping his voice low.

"Better than anyone expected. Dr. Hampton said that it's really a miracle that she is still alive. He was worried she wouldn't make it after being taken off the respirator. But she doesn't seem to have any respiratory problems now, so her chances of recovering from RDS completely are much better than they were before."

"Well, that sure is good to hear. I'll bet that's a great relief to both of you."

"It sure is," Josh said as he glanced over at Sarah, who was sleeping soundly in her porta-crib.

AFTER TWO SHOWS IN WASHINGTON, the show traveled to Arizona. Hannah was feeling a little better since Josh had gotten up a couple of times with Sarah. However, he was such a sound sleeper, more times than not, she still got up instead of waking him. Getting one or two nights of sound sleep a week was still better than none.

Their first show in Arizona was in Mesa, where they stayed at the Superstition Inn. Hannah followed Josh and the Whitney's into their poolside room.

"The sure is a nice place," Emilie said.

"Hey, Hannah. How about going for a swim? Looks like a nice pool." Josh said with enthusiasm.

"I don't know, sweetheart. Sarah needs a nap and— "

Emilie interrupted. "You kids go ahead. Lance and I will watch little Sarah."

Josh looked hopefully at his wife. "What do you say, honey?"

"Well, okay. Give me a few minutes to get ready." Hannah took her swimsuit out of her suitcase and went into the bathroom.

"Thank you for offering to watch Sarah. Hannah has been so tense and nervous lately.

"You two need some time alone together. Enjoy yourselves," Emilie said with a smile.

HANNAH WAS SITTING on the edge of the pool, letting her legs dangle the water, while Josh was waist-deep in water. They were alone in the pool. Hannah slid into the cool water next to him. "I'll sure be glad when we get home. I'm looking forward to some time off after this tour."

Josh held out his arms and pulled her towards him. "We can go and rent a cabin."

"Yeah, maybe," she replied. "Or just stay home, and rest. I'm tired of being away from home."

"Or that," he replied, not wanting to say anything that could result in another argument.

11 - SARAH'S SONG

*S*everal days later, the tour took them to Texas, their first show in Austin. Earlier, Mr. Whitney had impressed upon the performers and crew the importance of this show, as it was being filmed by the Gospel network to be considered for the upcoming slot hosting a national T.V. gospel show.

Hannah walked warily from their dressing room towards the side of the stage to wait for their entrance. She had a bad migraine come on a half-hour ago, which was a little better, after taking her pills for it, but still throbbing. Disjointed thoughts were running through her head. *I don't really want to perform tonight... so tired... Sarah...these headaches... pills. How many did I take? I can't miss this performance...* With her head still hurting, she took two more pills before rounding the corner to the side of the stage.

Josh was already at the side of the stage and interrupted her thoughts. "Feeling any better, honey?" He asked, taking her hand.

"A little," was all she could say. She needed to conserve her energy for singing. She heard the song being performed on stage, and Mr. Whitney began their introduction. When he finished, she and Josh walked to the center of the stage together. He was smiling and nodding to the audience's applause as he put his guitar strap around his neck.

The lights were blinding and made her head hurt worse. Halfway through the song, during her solo, she faltered, her mind suddenly going blank. Josh glanced at her in surprise at the first stumble, but when she stopped singing completely, he kept strumming his guitar as tried to think of a way to continue but realized he couldn't sing both their parts and make it work.

Hannah, unable to think clearly or to understand what was happening, had to get away. She quickly walked off stage and headed towards the dressing room.

Embarrassed, he muttered an apology to the audience and left the stage, while the T.V. cameraman looked at him questioningly. Lance appeared, wondering what was going on. Josh explained that she just walked off stage but didn't know why.

Lance told him to go check on her, while he went out on the stage to apologize to the audience and try to get the show back on track.

Josh, angry because he was worried they might have blown their chance at the T.V. show, strode towards their dressing room. He was just about to open the door when Emilie stopped him.

"Josh, I don't think you should try talking to her right

now while you're still so upset. Think about how she must be feeling right now."

"Mrs. Whitney, I have a real right to be angry. She just ruined our song in front of a thousand people and the T.V. crew. She knows how important this show is for all of us. I mean, it's bad enough we have Sarah's issues to deal with, and now this?"

"Josh, please let me talk to her. There's got to be an explanation as to why this happened."

"Oh, I think I know why––because she probably thinks that she'll get fired if she spoils the show."

Emily was shocked. "Joshua Bryton! I'm surprised at you. How could you think that your own wife would do that on purpose?"

Feeling a bit chastised, but still frustrated, Josh said, "Go ahead and talk to her, Mrs. Whitney, because right now, I don't think she will talk to me." With that, he walked away.

Emily knocked on the door to the dressing room. "Hannah? May I come in? It's me, Emilie." Hearing no response, she tried again. "Please let me in. Everything is going to be okay." When there was still no answer, Emilie knocked again. "Hannah?"

This time Hannah cautiously opened the door. "Where's Josh?" She asked wearily.

"I asked him to let me talk to you alone for a few minutes. Can I come in?"

Very softly, she said, "Okay." Hannah moved aside, allowing her to come in.

"What happened out there?" Emilie asked.

"I-I don't know," Hannah answered. "My-my mind just

suddenly went blank. All of a sudden, I-I couldn't remember the words. I looked over at Josh, and even he looked like a stranger. I couldn't even remember where I was." She was visibly shaking.

Emilie put her arms around Hannah to comfort her, realizing how scared she must be.

"Hannah, I know you would never do something like this on purpose. And I know how scared you must have been out there. Honey, please tell me what's going on with you. I want to help you if I can."

Hannah shook her head. "But-but I don't know what happened, Mrs. Whitney. "

"Honey, how did you feel when you went on?"

Hannah shrugged as she struggled to remember the moments before she walked out onto the stage. "I was tired. And I have a headache." She said. "But that's been normal lately."

"I think you've been under a great deal of stress these past few months and it's finally catching up with you. Maybe you just need to rest."

"I guess Josh is pretty mad at me," Hannah said. "And I don't blame him. I ruined our song, and probably everyone else's chances of getting the on the T.V. show. You know how much pride he takes in us being professional. He's never gonna forgive me for this."

"Oh, sure, he will," Emilie said, reassuringly. "And I'll take to Lance about the T.V. show. I'm sure we'll find a way to straighten things out with the network."

Hannah sighed heavily. "I hope you're right, Mrs. Whitney."

12 - SARAH'S SONG

*I*n their room, at the next leg of the tour, Hannah sat down on the edge of the bed with Sarah in her arms, still very tiny for her age. They had just arrived in Dallas. She watched in silence as Josh took a few things out of his suitcase. He'd hardly spoken to her since the night before. "Josh, can we please go out to mom and dads? We've got all day and— "

"We're not going anywhere." Josh interrupted. "After what happened last night, you don't need to be doing anything except spending the day resting here, just like Mr. Whitney said."

"But they're expecting us. I can rest at the ranch."

"No. It's at least an hour's drive, time that you could be resting. Call them and tell them we're not coming." Still angry, he was worried about how disappointed everyone in the cast would be if they lost the national T.V. show, and especially for himself and Hannah. Hannah felt hurt, but Josh failed to notice and said, "Sarah is sleeping, and you should be too. I'll be back later."

He stepped outside the room and went for a walk. He had to think.

He had always wanted to be on national T.V., singing the praises of the lord. But now, he wondered if they were being forsaken? *Why are we being tested like this?* For the second time in his life, the first being after they were told about Sarah's handicaps, he felt like God had abandoned them.

AFTER HE HAD GONE, Hannah picked up the phone and dialed the number to her parent's ranch. "Hi, mom," she said when her mother, Nora, answered the phone.

"Hannah, honey, what's wrong?"

Hannah started to cry. She told her mother all that had happened the night before during their show. She continued with, "Mom, Josh is really mad at me. He's barely speaking to me."

"Well, we'll talk about it when you get here. What time are you coming?"

"We're not. Mr. Whitney said I should spend the day resting, and Josh said that he wants me to stay here."

"Honey, this concerns me. It sounds like you were disorientated. And, why would Josh get so angry?

"I ruined our number in front of hundreds of people, and I'm sure it embarrassed him. Worse, he thinks we might lose the T.V. show chance because of it."

"Your dad and I had already planned to be at the show

tonight to surprise you. We are looking forward to seeing you both and meeting our new granddaughter. We can talk about it then."

"I can hardly wait to see you and daddy too."

"Okay, honey. You get some rest, and we will see you tonight."

"Bye, Mom." Hannah hung up and checked on her daughter, who was asleep in her porta-crib. She laid down, curled up on the bed, and fell asleep herself.

JOSH HAD COME BACK at 5 p.m. that evening and brought Hannah something to eat. He asked her if she got some sleep. She told him she did and had barely thanked him for the food when he told her he would see her onstage, obviously still not happy.

Hannah, still tired, ate the to-go meal, fed Sarah, and changed her. She got dressed and took Sarah to the dressing room, where she went back to sleep in her porta-crib.

Amber and the others left the dressing room to perform their skit. She finished her makeup and sat down on the couch to wait for the others to get back. They would watch Sarah while she and Josh did their songs. In a few minutes, she nodded off.

"HANNAH, WAKE UP!" Amber shook her. "You and Josh sing in five minutes… Hannah!"

"Oh." Hannah groaned. She forced her eyes open.

"Are you okay?" Amber asked.

"Y-yeah, I'm fine." Hannah got up, brushed her hair, took a couple of her pills as she felt another migraine coming on, and rushed out. She frantically reviewed the words to their song in her head. *I can't forget tonight,* she told herself. Her chest was tight, and she felt nauseous and dizzy after she joined Josh just offstage. She was glad for a moment to stop and catch her breath. Weak and shaky, her head was still hurting, she told herself, *only one more to go.*

She got through the song, despite her headache. It wasn't her best performance, but she hoped no one noticed.

After they walked off stage and were starting for the dressing rooms, Hannah halted, placing her hand on her temple. Josh stopped to look at her, puzzled. His expression changed from bewilderment to shock when her eyes rolled back into her head, and she collapsed towards him. He caught her with one arm, dropped his guitar, and carried her quickly into the dressing room. As he laid her down on a couch, his expression of worry alarmed the others in the room.

"Josh, what happened?" Kelly asked, a worried on her face.

"I don't know. She just collapsed." He took her head into his hands. She felt very warm, and her face was flushed. "Hannah...Hannah!" She didn't respond.

He pulled his hands away as Kristi brought some cold water and a towel and started dabbing her face with it.

Amber grabbed her wrist and took her pulse. After counting 15 seconds on her watch, she said, "Her pulse is fast, and her breathing is shallow. I think we better call an ambulance."

"I'll do it," Kelly said, pulling her phone out.

"I'll go find Lance and tell him," volunteered Kristi.

Josh had taken ahold of her hand, unable to say anything, not sure what to do.

The ambulance arrived, and Josh watched the paramedics check his wife's vitals. He answered their questions about what happened, her age, and her medical condition.

"Please tell me what is wrong," Josh said anxiously.

"Her heartbeat is fast," one paramedic answered. "We're going to take her to Dallas Medical Center." With that, the paramedics put her into the ambulance, closed the doors, and left the scene with sirens blaring, leaving a worried Josh.

He turned around and headed back inside to get Sarah and head to the hospital. As he approached the auditorium, he was surprised to see Hannah's parents, Steve and Nora, coming out the door, holding his daughter. They had gotten Sarah from Amber in the dressing room while Josh had followed the EMT's to the ambulance.

"Come on, Josh. We'll drive you." Steve said. Grateful, he followed them to the parking lot.

AT THE HOSPITAL, Josh pace nervously while the doctor examined Hannah behind a closed curtain in the emergency room. *What is wrong with her?*

After what seemed like an hour to Josh, the doctor came out. "Mr. Bryton? We've stabilized your wife. She'll be okay, but I'm admitting her to the hospital for observation and some tests." Dr. Marcus paused as he looked at his watch, then added, "She'll be taken to room 414. I'll be in to see her again soon. Meanwhile, please go with the nurse. You'll need to fill out some paperwork."

"Okay. Thank you, Dr.," Josh said, relieved. A nurse took him to admissions; he was handed a clipboard and told he could see his wife after he was finished.

When Hannah awoke a few hours later, she was lying in a hospital bed. *What am I doing here?* She wondered. As her vision cleared, she saw Josh sitting beside her, reading a magazine. "Josh?"

At the sound of her voice, he closed the Bible and said, "I'm right here, honey."

"W-what happened? Why am I in the hospital?"

"Do you remember what happened?"

Hannah shook her head, no.

"You collapsed right after we left the stage. We couldn't bring you around. You really had me scared."

"Sarah. Where is Sarah?" Hannah asked anxiously.

"She's with your parents back at the hotel. They stayed until the Dr. confirmed you'd be okay." Josh said.

"Josh, why am I here? What's wrong with me?"

"Dr. Marcus said that you are suffering from exhaustion." He paused and looked at her somberly. "Honey, he said you have drugs in your bloodstream. I told him that you're not taking any kind of drugs, but he said the blood test confirmed it. So, I looked in your purse—and I found these." Josh reached into his pocket and pulled out her prescription pill bottle for the headaches.

Hannah looked at the pills, then back at Josh. Then she looked away.

"What are they for? Why didn't you tell me?" He raised his voice as he continued, "You know how I feel about pills."

"They're for headaches. I––I needed them. And I didn't think you'd listen, so I decided it wasn't worth mentioning."

"You didn't think I'd listen? I always listen to you!" He couldn't believe she said that.

Hannah was silent for a moment, her frustration growing before answering. "No, Josh, you don't!" Angrily, she continued. "I tried to tell you right after we brought Sarah home that I didn't think I could work and care for Sarah. You wouldn't listen then. You didn't listen when I told you I was too tired to go over to Jeremy and Rachel's." Her throat was dry, but she decided to get it all out. "When I took Sarah to the clinic for a checkup, Dr. Hampton said that I should take a leave of absence for a while. That's when I started taking the pills. He prescribed them for my headaches. You didn't seem to notice or care that I wasn't feeling well. Worse yet, Mr. Whitney spoke with me and said that I was irritable and short-tempered. I asked him to be excused from this tour, but he talked me out of it because of the T.V. show, that with Leo and Aimee out, he wouldn't be able to fill out the show."

She glared at him as she paused for a sip of water, then continued. "And when I forgot the words to the song, you couldn't seem to yell at me enough. I-I don't know why that happened, but I was scared. When I forgot the song, I couldn't even remember where I was or who you were. You wouldn't listen when I tried to tell you that I didn't know why it had happened. You thought I had done it on purpose!"

She slammed her fist down on the bed. "I-I always thought I meant more to you than that." Feeling drained, she started to cry.

Josh, in shock at her outburst, opened his mouth to speak, but no words would come. The pained look in her eyes and the anger and disappointment on her face broke his heart.

"I should've realized right away last night when you stopped singing that something was wrong. Maybe if I listened to you, none of this would've happened." He was looking at the floor, shame on his face.

Hannah was wiping her eyes when Dr. Marcus came in. "I'm sorry, Mr. Bryton, but it's time for you to go. It's after midnight; you shouldn't even be here. Your wife needs to sleep." Josh didn't want to leave her, but he knew the Doctor was right.

"Ok. Honey, I'll be back in the morning. We can talk then. You need to get some rest." Hannah closed her eyes as the medication they had given her for sleep began to take effect. Josh kissed her. "I love you, sweetheart."

With that, he thanked the Doctor and left the room.

13 - SARAH'S SONG

*J*osh quietly entered the motel room, not wanting to wake the Whitney's, but they were still up. "I thought you'd be asleep."

"We were waiting for you. How is Hannah? What did the doctor say?" Emilie asked.

"They're still waiting on some of the test results." He was still thinking about what she had said about him, not listening. Josh looked down at his feet. "This is all my fault. This never would've happened if I'd listened to her."

"What you mean?" Lance said.

"I haven't been listening to her. Ever since we brought Sarah home, Hannah has said that she was too tired to go anywhere. She wanted to quit the show because she didn't think she could take proper care of Sarah and work such a hectic schedule." Josh paused to take a deep breath, then continued. "I told her that we'd do it together, but...well, she does it all. I made her promise not to quit. I was so used to the go-getter she usually is, I guess I just thought it was normal new mother stuff."

Lance looked uncomfortable. "Neither did I. She asked to be excused from this tour, but I talked her out of it," he said, regret in his voice.

Emilie shook her head. "I'm just as guilty as you both. Hannah wasn't feeling well when we first flew into Bellevue. I didn't think that she should perform that night, but she pleaded with me not to tell anyone. Now I wish I had insisted that she didn't."

"Give her a few days to rest." Lance suggested. "In fact, I think you need to take some time off to be with her."

"But, the T.V. show…"

Lance stood up and put his hand on Josh's shoulder. "I'll deal with the show. You need to be with her now. Take the rest of the week off. No arguments."

Josh sighed. "Well, maybe just this week."

THE NEXT MORNING, Josh entered Hannah's hospital room. She was awake.

"Hi, babe." He gave her a kiss.

"Hi. I suppose everyone is getting ready to go to Houston today."

"Everyone except me. I'm not going. Mr. Whitney excused me for the rest of this week."

"But you have to go. The T.V. network will be filming again. Maybe Amber can fill in for my part. I can stay with mom and dad until I'm well enough to fly home."

"No, honey. I'm *not* leaving you. I called your parents. We're going to stay with them until Dr. Marcus says it's okay for you to go home.

Hannah blinked back tears. "Did you tell Mr. Whitney where I am?"

"He'll stop by to see you later. He says he has something for you."

HANNAH FELT a lump in her throat when Mr. and Mrs. Whitney came into the room a short time later, worried that they would be upset about her forgetting their song a couple of nights earlier.

"Hello, Hannah," Emilie said as she smiled.

"These are for you," Lance said as he handed her a dozen yellow carnations.

"They're beautiful. Thank you."

"I must apologize, Hannah, for not excusing you from this tour. I didn't realize how serious the situation was."

"I'm sorry I forgot the song the other night. Josh was pretty angry. He had every right to be. So did you. I just wish I knew why it had happened. "Hannah said softly.

"Let that go, Hannah," Lance said. "Right now, the important thing is that you get some rest."

Emilie patted her on the shoulder. "We will see you later, Hannah. You need to sleep for a bit."

"Thank you for coming. It means a lot to me," she said.

LATER THAT AFTERNOON, Hannah was alone in the hospital room. She was glad to be alone. She had so many feelings to sort out. *Will Josh allow me to quit the show? How long will it take me to get my strength back? Will Josh now believe that I can't work and care for Sarah?* Hannah looked up as the door opened, and her parents came in.

"Hi, dear. How do you feel?"

"Still tired, but a little better than I've felt in quite a while. Did Josh come?"

"He's at the ranch. Sarah's sleeping. He'll be here later," her dad said.

Nora hugged her daughter. "He's pretty worried about you."

Hannah didn't reply but looked down.

"Listen, Hannah. He doesn't understand why you didn't tell him about the medication. I think you two need to have a talk. Tell him what you told us."

"I can't," Hannah answered. "He'll be mad because I kept it from him. And he has the right to be upset. I should've told him."

Steve was angry. "Honey, you said in your letters that he wouldn't listen. Now maybe he will. I'd like to-- "

"Daddy, please don't be angry at Josh. He didn't know— "

"He didn't know because he didn't listen."

"This is just as much my fault," Hannah whispered. "If I had told him about the pills, then maybe he would've agreed that I should take some time off."

"If he had listened to you in the first place, you wouldn't need the pills," Nora said.

Hannah sighed, then closed her eyes. "I really don't feel like talking about this anymore. I'm kinda tired."

"Alright, you get some rest, we'll come back later," her father said as he kissed her on the forehead.

14 - SARAH'S SONG

*S*teve paused in the doorway to the living room when he noticed Josh sitting there, talking on the phone. He started to move away and stopped as Josh said, "Yes, Mr. Whitney, I'm sure that she'll be able to stay here with her parents...they'll help with Sarah...I could rejoin you..."

Josh's conversation with Mr. Whitney continued, but Steve had heard enough.

He went outside and set off on a walk to think about the situation. When he got home, dinner was being served.

"Steve! Where have you been?" Nora asked.

"Sorry I'm late. I was out walking."

"Did you have a nice time?"

It was fine."

Something in his tone made Josh uneasy.

LATER THAT EVENING, while Josh put Sarah to bed, Steve rummaged through Nora's desk and found what he was looking for. He looked up and said, "Nora, I want to have a man to man conversation with Josh. Would you mind leaving us alone down here?"

"Of course not, dear." Nora went upstairs.

When Josh came down, he found Steve alone in the living room. Steve looked up and said, "Josh, I'd like to talk to you."

"Sure," Josh said as he sat down.

"I happened to overhear a little of your phone conversation earlier. Dr. Marcus thinks Hannah will be able to come home in a few days, and you're considering rejoining the tour. Is that right?"

"Uh—Yes. You see, we're all expected to tour. Mr. Whitney has released Hannah, but I have to honor my commitment. I was only given a week off."

"What about your commitment to your wife and daughter?"

"Well, that's why I am going. I have to provide for them, and the show is our livelihood, especially with the chance to be on national T.V. With Sarah's handicaps...well that would help make up for all the extra money we'll need for Sarah's care."

"To me, it seems Hannah is doing most of the care right now."

"For now, yes. But as Sarah gets older, she'll need a lot more special care."

"Josh, I want to speak very bluntly to you now. Please remember I love all of you and am concerned. That is the only reason I speak as I do. The fact is...Hannah needs you,

Josh. She fears that you are not truly concerned about Sarah's needs, that you're ashamed of her, and even that you don't love her—Hannah—because she gave birth to a handicapped daughter instead of a healthy child."

"You're kidding! Hannah knows better than that!"

"Does she now?"

"What do you mean?"

Steve picked up a pack of letters from the table. "These are letters Hannah has written to her mother and me since Sarah was born. I want you to read them and learn from Hannah what she's been thinking and feeling the last few months. Will you do that?"

"Well, sure, but…" Josh's voice trailed off.

"Read them," Steve said firmly. "Then, if you want to, I'll pray with you."

Josh nodded as he took the letters. After Steve left the room, Josh sat down on the couch and begin reading the first letter, which had been written only a couple of weeks after Sarah's birth.

Sarah hasn't shown much improvement. Sometimes, I feel so worn out. I can't bear to leave her, so I spend most of my time alone at the hospital. I know Josh has to work, but I wish he would spend more time at the hospital. I really need him there with me.

Josh continued reading the letters. As he read each one, he realized how much he had been hurting Hannah by not paying attention to her pleas about the problem she was having. By the time he had read the last letter, he was crying.

He looked up when Steve entered the room a while later, with shame on his face. "I didn't mean to hurt her, Steve. Really, I didn't. I guess I wasn't paying attention to her needs.

It all makes sense now… how can she ever forgive me? I've caused her so much pain."

"She'll forgive you, Josh, just as the Lord will. She loves you very much. That's why she never told you all the things she's told us. She didn't want to worry you. She didn't want you to read those letters, but I felt that you should know what's been going on with her."

HANNAH LOOKED UP WARILY when Josh walked into the room.

"Hi, honey." He said softly. "How are you feeling this morning?"

"A little better. How's Sarah?"

"She's fine. She loves grandpa and grandma. They've been giving her tons of attention, but I think she misses you." Josh sat down and took his wife's hand. "I want to talk to you seriously, Hannah— "

"I know you need to rejoin the tour. I'm awfully sorry about this, Josh— "

"No!" Josh shook his head. "I mean, yes, we will need to discuss that, but it's not what's on my mind this morning. He pulled up a chair and thought about how to tell her about his conversation with her dad the night before.

He sat down and took her hand in his own. "Your dad and I had quite a talk last night after Sarah was in bed. He gave me your letters to read. Is that really what you felt? What you believed—that I failed you and Sarah so miserably?"

"You weren't supposed to…why did dad…" She bit her

lip. "Yes," she admitted huskily. "That is what I believe. And I still do, Josh."

"I sure haven't given you any reason to believe anything else. I know saying 'I'm sorry' isn't much, honey, but I mean it. Sorry I have let you down so badly when you need my support more than ever. Hon...we dreamed to have a family, and I guess the thought of being on national T.V. was something I've always wanted. When Sarah came, all of that was shattered. I just didn't know how to cope. So, I withdrew and left you to struggle alone caring for a handicapped baby. I'm ashamed of how I treated you."

Hannah's eyes were wide, fixed on his face.

Josh's hand tightened on hers. "We've got Sarah, Hannah. God gave her to us for a reason. Josh smiled tenderly. "Last night, after Steve and I got through talking, I went and spent time with Sarah for a while. Handicapped or not, she's our baby, and I love her. From now on—for as long as she's with us— I'm committed to being with you to care for her. And after... Hannah, I love you. I want to give you all I can and receive from you all you have to give, even the doubts."

Hannah gently touched his cheek, speaking softly. "I love you too, Josh. I-I guess I really spoiled it for you."

"Honey, no one is blaming you. Everyone is very concerned about you."

"Dr. Marcus was in to see me a little while ago."

"Oh? What did he have to say?"

"He asked me how I've been feeling for the past few months. He said that in order for him to know exactly what was wrong, he needed to find out everything. I told him everything I could remember."

"And...?"

"He said that I have something called chronic fatigue syndrome."

"What is that? I've never heard of it."

"Some of the symptoms are dizziness, nausea, disorientation, headaches, and being tired all the time." She sighed, "and, he said the pills...they can cause some of the same symptoms. I guess I should have paid more attention to what the pharmacist said when I picked them up. Dr. Marcus was surprised that I made it as long as I did with a combination like that."

Josh was thoughtful for a moment. "That sure explains a lot."

"There's more...." Hannah said softly. "Before we went on stage...before I collapsed, my headache was extremely bad. So, I took more pills, thinking they would help. All I could think about was making it through our number..." Hannah's voice trailed off as she searched her husband's face.

Josh was silent for a few moments as he let her words sink in. "I am so sorry, darling. If it hadn't been for my self-ishness, you never would've needed those pills. You wouldn't be so worn out, and you wouldn't have collapsed. It's my fault for not seeing that something was wrong. When I think about what could have happened...you were right. I haven't been listening to you."

"Let's not talk about it anymore." Hannah's gentle smile reassured him that she forgave him.

"WE NEVER DID TALK about your rejoining the tour yesterday, Josh," Hannah said when he came into her room the next morning.

"I know. I talked to Mr. Whitney again. He needs an answer soon… if I am going to want more time off than the week he gave me."

"An answer? Oh—when you'll rejoin them?"

"Not exactly. I told him some of what you and me and Steve talked about. He wasn't too surprised. He already suspected there were problems between us surrounding Sarah's birth and disabilities." Josh paused before giving out the clincher. "He said that if I want to take some time off until you can rejoin, it's okay."

Hannah was stunned, just as Josh had been when Mr. Whitney had told him that. "He's making such a big exception," she murmured at last.

"Well, it helped that everyone else was in on it. They talked about it and went to Mr. Whitney. Amber and a couple others suggested some ways to rearrange the performances to cover for us, and Mr. Whitney approved, at least temporarily. But he cautioned me that if we get the T.V. show slot, and we couldn't be back before rehearsals for the filming started, we'd have to resign so he could look for a replacement for us. He was told they'd make a decision within a week, and if accepted, filming would start in a month after that." Josh paused before continuing. "He thinks we're going to get it. The producers said the show was great."

"Oh. I…" She hadn't considered that. All that hard work, all their dreams. What would they do then? "We have to…

But Dr. Marcus doesn't want me to tour at all now. He said what happened to me could happen again."

Josh was deep in thought. Torn between his love for Hannah and Sarah and losing the dream of what they'd always wanted. *Dear God, are you ever going to give us a break?*

Hoping they could find a way to continue, he said, "You could come along, and not perform. If I take up my share of the burden, maybe you could…we could manage."

Hannah frowned thoughtfully, considering that idea. Then she shook her head. "I don't know, Josh. Remember, you promised me once before, and…well, that didn't work out very well."

Josh sighed but didn't say anything.

"And, there'd be pressure," Hannah said doubtfully. "I would feel like I should be performing."

Josh nodded. "Hon, I have to know your opinion. Not what you think I should do, or what other people say, but what *you* want. Do you want us to go or stay?"

"We'd be letting Mr. Whitney, and all of our fans down if we… or at least you don't go."

"Maybe, but if I go, and you don't, I'll be letting you and Sarah down and fail in my responsibility as a father and husband. I won't do that again."

Hannah bit her lip. She looked at him with resignation on her face.

"I see…Well, that settles it. I'm staying. We'll leave it up to God." Josh lowered his head and said a silent prayer…

Even as much as I've had doubts about my faith lately, I have to learn to trust you again. Please forgive me, Lord.

He looked up at Hannah and said, "As soon as you're able,

we'll go home."

"Dr. Marcus said that I can be released tomorrow, but I have to stay in bed for a week, and he wants to see me again next Friday to make sure I can travel before we head home. He said I'll probably take three or four weeks to fully regain my strength, so I won't be able to work again for at least that long."

"You need the time off. I don't want anything like this to happen again. I was so scared when you collapsed. And those pills––"

"I needed those pills. My headaches were so bad, and I couldn't sleep at night. A couple weeks ago, I started getting sick to my stomach whenever I took them. I just figured it was the flu or something."

"I'm not blaming you. I just wish I would've known."

"I-I didn't think…I'm sorry." She didn't tell him she kept the pills. She was still afraid of the headaches.

"You have nothing to be sorry for. Everything will be fine. I promise. I've been trying to reconcile some things about my faith lately, trying to believe that if God wants us back on tour, he'll make it happen."

"You're right. I guess I should've considered that." She wouldn't admit it, not even to herself, but she had been… in fact was still angry at God and had only been paying lip service to the prayers the group. She hadn't actually prayed herself since, well, she couldn't remember right now. *After all you put us through, how could you blame me?* They had given her a different painkiller earlier, *but what if the headaches return?* She decided to keep the pills for a while, just in case.

15 - SARAH'S SONG

*M*om, Where's Josh?"

Nora looked up from the book she was reading. "He had to go into town."

"That figures," Hannah said, frustrated. She had tried to stop taking the migraine pills because of the side effects, and she had woken up with a throbbing headache. She took another pill, and the nausea had returned, and she was a little dizzy.

"What's that supposed to mean? And what are you doing out of bed?"

"I just got out of the hospital. I was hoping we could spend some time together. There are a lot of things we need to work out. Maybe he didn't mean what he said after all. He's probably mad because I didn't want him to rejoin the tour."

"Hannah, he'll be back soon. And I'm sure he meant what he said. He loves you.

"Yeah," Hannah said softly.

Nora could see the look of her in her daughter's eyes. She put her arms around Hannah and hugged her closely. "You'd better go back to bed. You know what Dr. Marcus said. I'll tell Josh to go up and see you as soon as he gets home."

"Don't bother. I don't care if he does or not."

JOSH WAS quiet as he entered the bedroom an hour later. A few minutes earlier, Nora had told him that Hannah felt hurt because he had gone into town instead of staying with her. He laid down on the bed beside her and put his arms around her. Hannah rolled over but remained silent. Josh kissed her lightly on the cheek. "Hi. Your mom said that I should come up to see you."

"I don't want you to feel obligated or something," Hannah answered bitterly. "I'm sure you have more important things to do."

Josh rubbed her cheek. "Honey, please don't be angry."

"Why shouldn't I be? All I want is for you to spend some time with me. We need to talk. I just got out of the hospital. Couldn't it have waited until tomorrow?"

"No, it couldn't, because I had to get this." Josh picked up a small box from the nightstand and handed it to her.

Hannah looked at him for a moment, then took the box. "What's this for?" She asked.

"Open it," Josh said.

Hannah opened the box and gasped. "Oh, Josh. They're beautiful." Suddenly, she felt bad for being so angry at him. When she looked up at him, her eyes were wet.

Inside the box was a diamond necklace shaped like a heart, with matching earrings. "Oh, Josh," she said again.

"Here," Josh said, handing her an envelope.

Hannah opened it and took out the card.

The entire card was covered with red roses, and inside it said...

There are not enough roses in the world to say how much I love you.

Then she read the words he had written...

To my darling Hannah, from this day forward, I promise to always listen to you, to always support you, to always be here for you, to always share in the care and the love of our daughter. My love for you will never die.

When she finished, she closed the card and gave him a hug. "I love you too, sweetheart. I'm sorry that I ever doubted your love for me—and for our daughter.

"I'm sorry I doubted you," he replied as he returned her hug.

Hannah was silent for a moment as she looked at him. His dark eyes were full of love and compassion. Hannah reached up and touched his cheek, whispering softly. "Sarah is sleeping, and I'm not supposed to get up. If you don't have anything else to do, how about keeping me company for a while?"

"I'd like that," Josh said as he slipped into bed beside her. Hannah snuggled close to him, enjoying the warmth of being held in his arms. For the first time in several months, she felt loved and secure.

After Hannah went to sleep, Josh got up and went downstairs. He found Steven and Nora sitting at the kitchen table.

"Hi, Josh," Steve greeted him. "How is Hannah doing?"

"She just wants to sleep. But she seems to be feeling a bit better."

"That's good to hear."

"Steve, I want to thank you for talking to me the other night. It really set me straight on a few things that I never would have known if you hadn't taken the time to share them with me."

"Well, I didn't want you to think that I was sticking my nose where it didn't belong, but Hannah is my daughter, and I didn't want to see her get hurt anymore. And Josh, you're like a son to us. I didn't want this to tear you and Hannah apart."

"I can promise you that nothing like this will ever happen again." Josh sat down at the table and said, "I've been thinking, I wonder if you could help me with something else?"

"Sure, "Steve replied. "What is it."

Josh said sheepishly, "I'm ashamed to admit it, but I've really had a crisis of faith lately. Would you and Nora pray with me?"

"Of course!" Nora and Steve both acknowledged.

They spent the next hour talking and praying together.

As they were reading a psalm, Hannah came down, smiling and said, "I woke up with a strange feeling, like I had to come down here. Now I see why. I've felt bad about it, but

I've been so angry at the Lord lately, and I think he's telling me it's time to trust him again."

Josh smiled and held out his hand to her and said, "I've felt the same way; after I left you upstairs, I felt an over-whelming need to pray and asked your mom and dad to join me. And now you too!" He pulled out a chair for her, and they all bowed their heads and gave their thanks.

JOSH AND HANNAH walked into Dr. Marcus's office on Friday morning, nine days after Hannah had collapsed.

Dr. Marcus opened Hannah's file and read it silently for a moment, then looked at the young couple sitting before him. "How have you been feeling, Mrs. Bryton?"

"Much better. I still tire easily, but I've been getting a lot of rest. Josh and my parents have been taking care of Sarah. I still get the headaches once in a while, but they're not as bad."

"That's good to hear. You look much better too. I think you can go home whenever you're ready. Under the circumstances and to prevent this from happening again, Mrs. Bryton, I feel it might be best if you quit your job, at least for a while. It will take quite a while for you to fully recover."

Josh nodded. "I think you're right, Dr. Marcus. Working and caring for Sarah puts her under too much pressure."

"And Mr. Bryton, your wife will need a lot of help, especially the next few weeks while she's recuperating."

Josh reached over and held his wife's hand. "Dr. Marcus, this happened because I neglected my duties as a husband and father. I didn't listen when she tried to tell me what her needs were. A child's birth is supposed to bring a couple closer together, but Sarah's birth pulled us apart as we each tried to deal with it our own way. Not only did we drift apart from each other, but we also drifted apart from the Lord as well. He used this experience to bring us closer to Him and closer to each other."

Hannah nodded. "The Lord is showing us that we need to communicate with each other, and we need to turn this over to him."

Dr. Marcus smiled. "You two are a very remarkable couple. To tell you the truth, I often pray for my patients."

"NEED ANY HELP, DEAR?" Nora stood in the doorway of Josh and Hannah's room.

"No, thanks, mom. I'm almost done. Where's Josh?"

"He's downstairs with Sarah. Are you sure you want to leave today?"

Hannah sighed as she sat down the bed. Nora sat down beside her. "I love being here, mom. It's just that I think we need time to work things out. You know, caring for Sarah as a team...and spending time together."

"You're right, Hannah. But we sure enjoyed having you here. Maybe in a few weeks, your dad and I can fly out to California."

"That be great, mom. By then, I'll be myself again."

Nora put her arms around her. "Call us if you need us. And honey, please talk to Josh if problems arise. He loves you so very much."

INSPIRING SPECIAL NEEDS STORIES

"I know he does," Hannah answered. "I love him very much too." Hannah closed her suitcase, then glanced quickly at her watch. "I guess I'd better go. Our plane leaves in a couple of hours, and it takes almost an hour to get to the airport."

Nora hugged her again. "We'll be praying for you, dear. Everything will be fine now.

"I know it will, mom. Thank you for everything. If it hadn't been for you and daddy-- "

"And the Lord," Nora added. "The Lord works through us."

"I know. And I'm glad he did."

Nora picked up the suitcase and followed her daughter downstairs.

16 - SARAH'S SONG

*J*osh had left for work, and Hannah smiled to herself as she rinsed off the morning dishes after feeding Sarah. Today was April 24, and little Sarah was exactly 7 months old. She had surprised everyone, especially the doctors, by making it this long.

The past several weeks had been a struggle for her as she fought to regain her own strength, but with the help of her husband, their many friends, and God, she was now able to do the housework and care for Sarah. She still tired easily and would need to rest often during the day. The T.V. network had offered the Whitney's the slot, and even though he had to hire a replacement act for them, he offered Josh a job planning rehearsals and writing new material. Since she was feeling more confident about her ability to take care of Sarah, they prayed about it and decided he should accept the job. The studio was about a forty-five-minute drive, and he wouldn't have to travel. He even said he could probably use their act back in as backup if they decided they were up to it in the future. She and Josh decided together that it would be best if she didn't go back to work, at least not for a while.

AS SHE TURNED the water off, she heard a funny little gasp from Sarah. She turned around, half-smiling because she often made funny noises like that. The smile vanished instantly when she saw Sarah's mottled face and heard her raspy breathing.

Sarah? What's wrong? Are you choking? No! Hannah dropped what she was doing and ran over to her daughter.

She snatched Sarah out of the highchair and tried to think of what could be wrong. Putting her finger in Sarah's mouth, she couldn't feel any food. She was starting to turn blue as she continued to struggle for breath. Panicked, she ran to the phone and dialed 911.

"Hello...yes, I need help! My baby daughter can't breathe...she's turning blue! I don't know what...no, I checked, and she's not...no, I don't know...I fed her, and a few minutes later she started gasping...her breathing is really raspy...please send an ambulance..." Hannah gave them the address and hung up. She wrapped Sarah in a blanket then hurried outside to wait for the ambulance. *What could be wrong?*

The two attendants met her halfway up the walk. They took Sarah and placed her in the back of the ambulance, checking her vitals. Hannah listened to their comments with growing terror as she got in to ride with them.

"Pulse is erratic. Fast, slow, thready. Now I can hardly get it."

"BP is dropping."

"I'm putting in a respiratory tube—she can't breathe."

"Convulsions aren't slacking."

BY THE TIME they reached the hospital, Sarah was in a coma. Hannah had given them Dr. Hampton's name on the way. He was waiting when the ambulance pulled in and began examining Sarah as she was wheeled into the emergency room. The two ambulance attendants reported their observations and treatment.

Hannah helplessly watched the flurry of activity around her little daughter.

A nurse approached her. "Can you give me some information, Mrs. Bryton? Tell me what happened?"

"Okay..." Hannah was still staring at them, working on Sarah.

"What did she eat?" The nurse persisted.

She looked at the nurse, her face ashen. "Uh—Some cereal. It was fairly thin. She chokes otherwise. And...and some strained fruit."

"Mixed fruit?"

"Uh—No. Cherry, I'm trying different kinds of fruits."

"What kind of cereal?"

"Mixed. Yes, that's right. Mixed."

"She'd had it before?"

"Oh, yes. Quite a few times."

"So, the Cherry was new?"

"Yes."

The nurse nodded. "That's all for now, Mrs. Bryton." She went and spoke quickly and quietly to Dr. Hampton. Hannah could see his frown. He gave the other nurse some orders, then came over to Hannah.

"Sarah is in a coma, Mrs. Bryton. We've put her on a respirator—she's not breathing on her own. Her pulse is very weak, and her blood pressure is quite low. There is no response to stimuli—not a very good report, I'm afraid."

Hannah turned white. "Is Sarah dying?" She asked.

Dr. Hampton nodded. "We're doing all we can, but I'm afraid Sarah is beyond our help. I think you better call your husband and have him come."

"Yes, I will. You'll keep her alive till then?"

"We'll do our best."

Hannah looked over toward Sarah, then took her phone out to call Josh. While she was dialing, they moved Sarah to a room off of the ER. Hannah followed them and watched them hook up the monitors. Hannah stood beside her, watching and waiting.

Josh found them there when he arrived 45 minutes later.

Dr. Hampton met him on his way in and stopped him long enough to say, "It's only a matter of time, Mr. Bryton. We can't say for sure what happened— possibly a severe allergic reaction to something she ate—but it doesn't look good. The life support is keeping her alive now. You and your wife are going to have to decide. Do you want us to keep her on life support—prolonging her life—or take her off?"

"If you took her off— "

"I don't think she'd last long, Mr. Bryton, even if she did, the lack of oxygen—there is likely severe brain damage."

Josh nodded slowly. "I'll talk to Hannah." He walked into the room. "Honey, I'm here."

Hannah looked up, sobbing, and said, "She's... our little girl is dying."

"I know. Dr. Hampton told me—" He choked, unable to continue for a moment, and then said, "He said we have to make a decision— "

Hannah interrupted; her voice fierce. "I want her off all this stuff. She's dying, and it's senseless to try to hang on to her this way."

"Are you sure?" Josh whispered.

She nodded. "I don't want her to die," she said softly. "But to live like this...no."

As tears continued to stream down her face, she turned to cling to Josh. He held her close as he cried, too. Then, keeping one arm around Hannah, he reached over to touch Sarah's head while he prayed out loud...

"Dear Lord, you know we love our little girl with all our hearts. Please, Lord, comfort her...take away her pain...bless her with all of your love...and comfort us in our time of sorrow. We thank you for the time we've had with her...for all you and she have taught us. We will cherish her memory forever...in your name, we pray. Amen."

As he hugged Hannah tightly, he pushed the call button. Dr. Hampton came immediately.

"We can't let her live like this," Josh said. "We want you to take her off life support."

"Are you both sure?" Dr. Hampton asked.

"Yes. It would be selfish of us to try to hang on to her like this. God gave her to us seven months ago, and now He is calling her home."

"Very well. "Dr. Hampton was silent as he unhooked the machines, then he gently picked Sarah up and placed her in her mother's arms. "Call me if you need anything. I will leave you alone with her."

Josh nodded, unable to say anything.

As Hannah held their dying child, she slowly rocked back and forth, softly singing 'Jesus loves me.' Josh led his wife over to the nearby rocking chair. Hannah sat down, holding little Sarah close.

Josh knelt down beside the chair, and with one arm around his wife and his other hand holding the tiny hand of his daughter, he prayed...

"Lord, we thank you for blessing us with this child. She brought us so much love and happiness. We now give her back to you."

Josh leaned over and kissed Sarah's soft cheek.

Hannah silently watched her daughter's chest rise and fall as she struggled with each breath. Finally, little Sarah Joylynn Bryton gave one last breath, then was still. "Our baby is with Jesus now," Hannah whispered.

Josh pushed the call button, and Dr. Hampton came in, followed by a nurse. "She's gone," Josh whispered.

Dr. Hampton checked for a heartbeat and found none.

"I'm sorry, Mr. and Mrs. Bryton. Would you like me to take her?"

Hannah pulled her closer. "Please, may we have a little more time with her?"

"Take as much time as you need," Dr. Hampton answered gently. "Call me when you are ready."

"Thank you," Josh answered. For the next half an hour, Josh and Hannah silently held onto their baby, knowing that once they let her go, it would be the last time they would hold her, and neither of them was ready to say goodbye.

"It's time, Honey." Josh said, "We need to let her go."

Hannah nodded and whispered, "I know." Tears flowed down her cheeks as she stared down into the face of her daughter. "Goodbye, my sweet Angel. I will love you forever."

Hannah gently handed Sarah to her father.

Josh kissed her on the forehead.

"Goodbye, Precious. Daddy loves you." Once again, Josh pushed the call button. This time, for the last time. Dr. Hampton returned.

Josh and Hannah held each other tightly as they left the room.

17 - SARAH'S SONG

hree weeks later, Hannah sat alone in Sarah's bedroom. They had a service for her, and it was standing room only in the church. In a portrait on the wall above the dresser was the three of them, taken shortly after Sarah had come home from the hospital, the only family portrait they had.

Lost in her own thoughts, she didn't hear Josh come into the room until he spoke.

"Hon? Are you okay?" He asked gently.

"I miss her so much. Sometimes at night, I can still hear her crying."

Josh walked over and put his arm around her. "Me too."

Hannah turned to face him, tears running down her cheeks. "I can't help but wonder if maybe I could've done something...then maybe she— "

"There's nothing you could've done. You heard what Dr. Hampton said."

The cause of her death had been determined to be a severe allergic reaction to something she had eaten.

"Maybe if I hadn't given her food that she hadn't had before— "

"Honey, you didn't do anything to cause her death."

"Then why do I feel so responsible? Like I did something wrong?"

"I know it's hard. But she lived longer than anyone thought she would. And she gave us so much. I guess she did the job that God sent her here to do."

"But we loved her so much. It's just not fair. She was only a baby. And she suffered so much."

"She'll never suffer again," Josh whispered. "She's a healthy child now."

"Every night, when I close my eyes, I can see her. I can hear her crying. I can see her smile."

"I know you haven't been getting much sleep lately. Why don't you lie down and rest for a while?"

"Yeah, I think it will. What are you going to do?"

"I think I'll mess around with my guitar for a while."

JOSH WAS SITTING on the couch, playing his guitar when the doorbell rang.

"Hi, Mr. and Mrs. Whitney. Come on in." They followed him into the living room. "Can I get you some coffee?"

"That would be nice, thank you." The Whitney's and Josh went into the kitchen, and Josh served them each a cup of coffee.

"Josh, we stopped over to see how you and Hannah are doing. We haven't seen much of you in the past few weeks."

"We're doing okay, I guess. It's hard, though. Sarah meant the world to us, and it's hard not having her with us."

"How is Hannah doing? Where is she, by the way?"

"She's sleeping right now. She hasn't been sleeping much at night, and she's been kind of withdrawn. She blames herself for everything. I'm really worried about her. She hardly leaves the house at all."

"Just give her time. I know she will be fine. I know the past seven months have been very difficult for her— both of you. Just remember that you need to work together."

"I found some Bible verses that might help you," Emilie said as she pulled a piece of paper out of her purse. "Read them with Hannah."

"Thank you. I've been searching the Scriptures, but I haven't been able to talk to Hannah about it. How can I help her?"

"Pray for her. Be there for her. Encourage her to talk about her feelings. She needs to talk about Sarah. And she has to realize that what happened is not in any way her fault."

"I'll do that Mr. Whitney; I've been thinking about returning to work pretty soon. I would like your permission to do a new song that I've just written. I would like Hannah and me to do a special performance of it, but I haven't asked her yet. It might be too much right now."

"I'm sure it would be fine. When can we hear it?"

I could sing it for you now if you'd like."

"I'd like that very much."

Josh, Lance, and Emilie went into the living room. Josh sat down on the couch and picked up his guitar. "I wrote this song the day of Sarah's funeral after everyone had left, and Hannah and I were home. Hannah had gone upstairs. I was sitting alone, thinking about Sarah...her birth, her life, and her death. Josh paused for a moment, then continued, "As I was sitting there, these words came to me. I call it 'Sarah's Song.'"

Lance and Emilie listened as Josh sang. They could see the pain in his eyes, and it was hard for him to sing the song.

"That was beautiful."

They turned to see Hannah standing at the bottom of the stairs.

"It sure was Josh," Lance said. "Are you sure you want to sing it on the show?"

"Yes. I want people to know what a blessing she was to us. She was a gift from God. And she gave us so much joy during her short life."

"And we learned so much," Hannah said softly. "She taught us how important it is for us to work as a team. And that we need to put our trust totally in the Lord and not try to carry our burdens alone.

"Speaking of the Lord, Mrs. Whitney suggested these bible verses for us," Josh said as he handed the paper to Hannah.

Hannah picked up her Bible from the coffee table. "Thank you. I like to read them out loud if it's okay."

"Of course," Emilie said. "We'd love to hear them."

Hannah read...

"2nd Corinthians 1:3-5. Praise be to God and the father of our Lord Jesus Christ, the father of compassion and the God of all comfort, who comforts us in all our troubles so that we can comfort those in any trouble with the comfort we ourselves have received from God. For just as the sufferings of Christ flow over into our lives, so also through Christ, our comfort overflows."

Hannah closed the Bible, her arms holding it tightly against her chest. "We want people to know that Sarah has taught us that we are never alone, not even during a crisis such as the death of a loved one. And, we want them to know that there is someone they can turn to, someone that will always be there for them and will always comfort them. The healing will be a long process, but we're not alone. God will heal our hearts."

"You're right, Hannah," Emilie said.

"Sarah will always have a very special place in our hearts. We can witness to others about our tragedy. We've gotten so much help from you two, our friends, and we've gotten cards of support from people we don't even know. And it has meant so much to us."

LATER, after the Whitney's left, Hannah lay awake that night, after Josh had gone to sleep. Gently weeping, she thought about Sarah. She missed her daughter very much, and the pain was unbearable at times, but she knew that with the Lord's help they would be okay.

Dear Lord, she prayed silently. Thank you for giving us Sarah.

Thank you for all you've done for us. Thank you for your comfort in our time of grief. Please help us to witness to others who are having their own painful experiences. In Jesus' name, amen.

Hannah closed her eyes and drifted into a peaceful sleep.

THE END

THANK you for reading my stories.

I deeply appreciate it and hope that if you liked them, you'll consider leaving a review.

Rena Yeager

ABOUT THE AUTHOR

Rena Yeager was born in Washington State and raised in Northern Minnesota. She discovered a passion for writing at the age of 14, in the mid-70s.

In the year 2000, Rena discovered the world of Fan Fiction and for the next several years, wrote many stories on the popular site Fan Fiction.

(https://www.fanfiction.net/u/50437/Rena)

After graduating college, Rena worked in the field of child-care, including co-owning a daycare center. In 1995, Rena made a career change and, for the past 25 years, has devoted her life to working with people with disabilities, both in their home setting and the Special Olympics.

Rena lives in Northern Minnesota with her Yorkie, Lexi.

Visit Rena's blog at:

https://www.alaskadp.com/rena-yeager-blog

And her social media sites:

facebook.com/Rena-Yeager-109220577620189

twitter.com/RenaYeager

pinterest.com/ryeager1961

instagram.com/ryeager1961

Made in the USA
Monee, IL
17 October 2020